North Wales Cinemas
Past and Present

Alan Phillips

Gwasg Carreg Gwalch

Published by Gwasg Carreg Gwalch,
12 Iard yr Orsaf, Llanrwst, Wales LL26 0EH
tel: 01492 642031
website: www.carreg-gwalch.cymru

Acknowledgements

A special thanks to Roger Ebert's of Cinema
Treasures and all contributors to the web site:

Also to Brian Hornsey and his vast knowledge
of cinemas in the country:
Abergele Library; Amlwch History;
Angelfire.com; Arthur Lloyd.com;
British Independent Cinemas Association;
Cinema Treasures; Cineworld Cinemas;
Coflein; Colwyn Bay Library; Daily Post;
Denbigh Archives; Gaumont Plaza Flint;
Gwynedd Archives;
Kinematograph Magazines and Year books;
Mercia Cinema Society;
National Media Museum, Bradford;
National Library of Wales, Aberystwyth;
Odeon Cinemas; Over the footlights.com;
RCHAMW; Rhyl Journal; Rhyl Life;
Service Sound and Vision Corpoation;
Silver Screen Archives;
Various North Wales Libraries; Wales on Line;
Welsh Cinema Photo History; (Facebook)
Wetherspoon J D; Wrexham History.

Also many thanks to various individuals, past
projectionists, managers and individuals that
worked in the cinemas who have contributed
valuable information and photographs.

A replica of a Bioscope Electric Cinema

Contents

Introduction

Cinemas have been a major part of people's lives for a number of years and most have wonderful personal memories of their 'local flicks'. Weekly visits to the local cinema or 'fleapit' as they were often refer to was an adventure and the only form of entertainment available. It was chance to step back in time or to the future, a chance to forget the daily toils and for an hour or two transported to a make believe world. Many made new friends and were an opportunity to meet once or twice a week. Others met their husbands or wives at a film show. By today the local cinema has more or less completely disappeared and people have to travel a great distance to see a particular film. Admittedly the multiplexes that have risen with their comfortable seating offer a choice of at least six or seven different films in their various screens and perhaps driven the small independent cinemas out of business. But thankfully there are still some individual cinemas left in north Wales, mostly ran by local authorities with the help of dedicated volunteers.

In the early years of the cinema, Town halls and Assembly rooms became the venue for the travelling film shows throughout Wales. North Wales had its own film pioneers such as John Codman son of the Llandudno Punch and Judy man who from the town's pier travelled throughout north Wales with his magic lantern living picture show. Perhaps the most re-known pioneer was Arthur Cheetham who filmed day to day scenes throughout the north for the purpose of showing them in venues around north Wales. Eventually settling in Rhyl and establishing the first permanent cinema. Regarded as Wales first film maker made approximate 30 short films including his first film Children playing on Rhyl sands in 1898, Royal Visit to Conwy (1899) and Buffalo Bill Cody visit to Rhyl in 1903. Another pioneer was J R Saronie a keen photographer from Liverpool who had developed an interest in cinematography, built up his business during the First World War touring the area showing films. He settled in the Prestatyn area establishing cinemas in the town and eventually ran three cinemas altogether in

1. Wadbrook's Royal Electrograph often visited the fairgrounds; 2. Arthur Cheetham Film Show (via Rhyl Library)

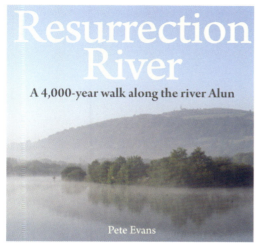

Resurrection River

A 4,000-year walk along the river Alun

Pete Evans

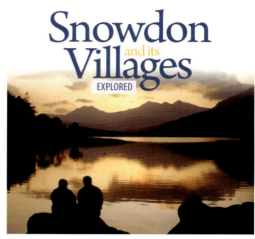

Snowdon
Villages *and its*
EXPLORED

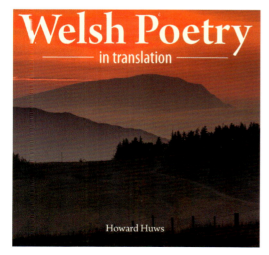

Welsh Poetry
in translation

Howard Huws

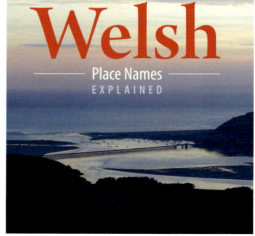

Welsh
Place Names
EXPLAINED

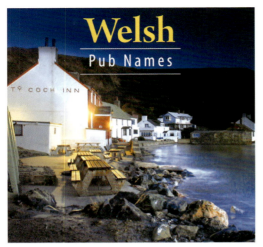

Welsh
Pub Names

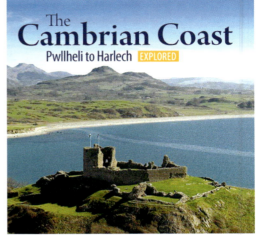

The
Cambrian Coast
Pwllheli to Harlech EXPLORED

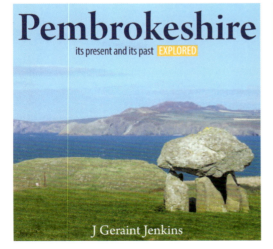

Pembrokeshire
its present and its past EXPLORED

J Geraint Jenkins

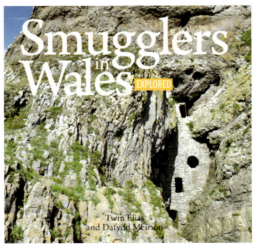

Smugglers
in
Wales EXPLORED

Twm Elias
and Dafydd Meirion

north Wales, Scala Prestatyn, City and Plaza in Bangor. These early venues were very primitive; the screen was usually a white canvas sheet or even a white painted wall while the projector was in the auditorium with the audience. Many were theatres and music halls utilised for film shows. However with the Cinematograph Act of 1909/10 halls had to obtain a licence to operate. Layouts of the halls had to change, projector boxes had to be away from the audience preferably in an enclosed fire resisting enclosure. One must remember film stock was made of nitrate and was highly flammable.

As the result several halls failed the stringent rule introduced and closed but others did survive and flourished and established themselves in the various locations. Several cinemas with more lavish auditoriums were built pre-World War 1, but most were built in the twenties and thirties. These were large buildings with impressive façade and auditoriums.

Over the years great strides were made in cinematograph, nitrate film were replaced with a safety film, the silent projectors were replaced by sound on disc and eventually by proper sound system on the film, colour films were introduced in

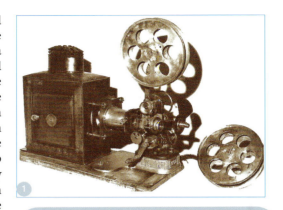

1. Pre 1900 cinema projector; 2. Kalee 8 projector with sound on disc (Silver Screen Archives)

thirties and in the fifties the advent of cinemascope (a process in which special lenses used to compress a wide image into a standard frame). New projectors emerged replacing the hand cranking machines of the early 1900s and the pre thirties equipment which could show films in stereophonic and some cinemas were equipped with 70mm equipment. Today in most cinemas the 35mm projectors has been replaced by 4K Digital projectors, capable of showing the latest films and live stage performances from round the world. Those towns that are fortunate to have multiplexes in their areas, choices of films have increased considerably.

With the advent of television and the increase running costs, cinemas attendances declined and most were converted for bingo but that too declined and the buildings closed and eventually were demolished.

However, by the sixties cinema attendances declined considerably and several went into financial difficulty, some cinema/theatres were converted into bingo halls, but were eventually used for other uses or demolished. Most were converted into supermarkets or some other retail business, but they too were eventually demolished. Today several cinemas have been taken over by J D Weatherspoon pubs that have retained their cinema or theatre décor to give us a glimpse of their glory days.

In North Wales most of the cinemas were independently owned as Wales had its entrepreneurs from the early days of cinematography. Saronie was listed has having three cinemas in north Wales in 1930s. The largest cinema chain was Mr Guy Baker's Paramount Picture Theatres Ltd based at Clive Building, Welshpool. By 1960 his company ran 16 cinemas throughout North Wales, but with his death in 1983 some of the cinemas closed for good; others were taken over by different proprietors. Another was EH James' Llanrwst Cinemas Ltd who ran six cinemas at various times in the area. In 1967 the Wedgewood Cinemas Ltd was formed and took over cinemas in Abergele, Colwyn Bay, Denbigh, Flint and Queensferry. Other cinema chain was run by the Deeside Enterprise Ltd. The two large UK companies, Odeon and ABC had only cinemas in Colwyn Bay, Llandudno, Rhyl and Wrexham.

1. Abergele, Conwy

The first cinema in the town dates back to around 1911 when the town and the area were visited by the travelling cinematograph shows. The venue was most probably the Town Hall as it was given a licence by Flint Town Council in January 1912 to hold film shows Monday to Saturday but not on a Sunday.

By 1920 films were regularly shown at the Town Hall with one show per night with two performances on Thursdays and Saturdays. The venue became known as the Empire Cinema ran by Messrs Mather and Smith and could accommodate 350 people.

Film shows had become popular entertainment in a small place like Abergele so Palace Theatre Company built a wooden structure in Market Street. Films were shown on the same basis as at the Empire but there were two film changes each week. Soon afterwards film showing in the Town Hall ceased. However on Thursday 12th November 1925 the wooden structure burnt to the ground as the result of a fire in a photo studio next door.

For the next few years there were no cinema facilities in Abergele but plans were drawn up and presented to a town meeting in March 1927 involving alterations to the town hall with an addition of a projection box on the outside of the building and new entrance in Market Street and a seating capacity for 400. The Abergele Entertainments Ltd was created and registered in May 1927 and the cinema was leased to a Mr Robert Roberts. Two performances were held nightly. In the thirties the sound system was improved by the fitting of AWH sound system.

During the war years 1939-45 as with most cinemas film shows ceased. In 1946 the running of the cinema was taken over Mr G E A James owner of the Llanrwst Cinema Company who renamed the venue the **Town Hall Cinema** and eventually the **Luxor**. In 1955 with the introduction of Cinemascope the proscenium of 15 feet had to be increased to at least 22 feet. New British Thomson-Hudson projectors and sound system was installed

From 1960 the cinemas was ran by a new lease holder based in Liverpool who changed the name yet again to the **Glyn**.

Before the end of the decade the Wedgewood Cinema Company of Colwyn Bay took over the lease and continued to run the cinema until part of the floor collapsed in 1970. The derelict structure remained empty but was eventually converted into shops.

1. *The Glyn Cinema Market Street, Abergele (via Abergele Library); 2. Luxor Cinema Abergele in 1952 (via Abergele Library)*

2. Amlwch, Anglesey

Amlwch, situated on the northern coast of Anglesey had two cinemas but not particularly at the same time.

The first in the early 1920s was the **Shannon** built by a Mr D Shannon. According to Kinematograph Year book the manager was listed as a Mr E Norgrove. The cinema showed one performance per night with a programme change twice a week with matinees shown on Wednesday and Saturday afternoons. Cinema seating was 270. In the twenties the cinema was taken over by C W and F L Johnson and in 1926 by a Mr Thomas Burrows. In 1930 the cinema was taken over once again by Mr W Lee who renamed the cinema – the **Lee Cinema**. The new owner spent a large amount of money refurbishing the building and installing a new Marshall Sound System but within six years the cinema closed.

A new purposely built cinema opened in July 1937, the **Royal** built by Mr T F Jones of Llangefni. The cinema had a 29 foot proscenium and seating capacity for 400. It was equipped with brand new Kalee 11 projectors and sound system. In 1955 a 29 foot Cinemascope screen was installed and the Kalee projectors were upgraded to take the new ratio lens. There was a one show per night, Monday-Saturday with two film changes per week. In 1966 the cinema closed due to poor attendance and the lack local support. The building was sold and converted into a Kwik-Save supermarket. It was sold again in 1995 and was acquired by the Co-op group who demolished the building and built a new store plus housing.

1. *Royal Cinema Amlwch taken in the fifties; 2. Royal Cinema in the 1980s as a supermarket; 3. Site of the Royal Cinema as it is today*

3. Bagillt, Flintshire

This is a small town on the north Wales coast situated beside the coastal road and the railway line.

The first cinema was the old **Foresters Hall** built as Working Men's Institute which opened its doors in September 1879. It is believed that the first cinematograph films were shown in the hall around 1908. As the result of the Cinematograph Act of 1910 the building was adapted for film showing as in 1912 with a projection room built on the outside with access by a

wooden stairs on the side of the building. By 1924 there was one performance per night and the programme was changed twice a week, but within a year film shows ceased and the cinema was closed.

It was not until 1936 that Bagillt got another cinema when a converted chapel on the High Street, built around 1810 was bought and converted into a cinema. The new cinema was called the **Regent** and had a seating capacity for 650. It was fitted with A.W.H projectors and sound system. Like most places of entertainment the cinema closed during the war years but opened again in 1946.

In the 1950s the cinema was ran by Messrs E V and N Davies in conjunction with the Grand Cinema in Flint. The cinema continued to show one performance per night.

With the advent of television in the fifties, cinema attendance declined and in a small village had drastic effect. In 1958 the building was changed to a licenced club with the stalls seating removed. It was converted to bingo and later to a store and yet another club.

After a period of uncertainty the building was bought by two individuals Messrs Moore and Blackmore with a view of transforming the derelict building into a cinema. The balcony was renovated as a 193 seater cinema and was opened on 15th November 1991 with a new name of the **Focus**. Seats for the cinema were acquired from the Gaiety Theatre Rhyl. Projectors and sound system came from Bristol while the 37 foot screen came from Margate. Everything looked rosy for the cinema as it was well supported but in 1995 it closed with arrest of the owner Peter Moore for murder. It was reopened for a brief period but finally closed in June 1996. Because of its recent history the building was demolished

Regent/Focus Cinema Bagillt closed before demolition

4. Bala, Gwynedd

In recent years Bala has become a tourism around Llyn Tegid (Bala Lake)which is the largest natural lake in Wales.

Victoria Hall on Pensarn Road, Bala was opened by Queen Victoria in 1890 and in the early 1900s it was often visited by the travelling Bioscope shows. The first talkie picture was shown in 1927. In 1930 the Victoria was listed as a 350 seat cinema which had a proscenium of 15 feet wide and was equipped with BTP (British Talking Pictures) projectors and sound system.

In 1950 the cinema was taken over by Guy Barker's Paramount chain showing three performances daily but by the end of the decade had been reduced to one. In 1970 with financial support from Bala Council the projection equipment was up dated by installing two Cinemeccanica Victoria 8 projectors and Western Electric sound system. In 1974 it was renamed **Neuadd Buddug** and during the eighties it closed again for alteration and decorating. The balcony was solely used as a cinema and the ground floor for other functions. With the death of Guy Barker in 1983 the cinema closed but was reopened and showed films three nights a week Wednesday, Fridays and Saturdays the other nights were devoted to other functions. It ceased showing films on 1st April 2015 when supply of 35 mm films became scares. For the next few years dedicated volunteers conducted a fund raising scheme so they could acquire a digital projector. Within 12 months, together with a grant from the Arts Council were able to acquire a digital projector.

1. Neuadd Buddug sinema Bala as it is today; 2. Neuadd Buddug auditorium (courtesy of the venue)

5. Bangor, Gwynedd

Bangor a university city had several cinemas over the years to cater for the students studying in the town. The earliest cinema in the town was a place referred to as the Palace which was seemingly the Town Hall. According to local history all film shows ceased at the **Palace** with outbreak of the First World War. Another early recorded venue was the Electric Pavilion which was run by a Mr W Summerson from around 1910 but changed its name to the **Picturedrome** in 1913. The 400 seat cinema was situated on the High Street more or less on the site of the Plaza years after. In 1914 it changed its name to the **Codman's Cosy Corner Picturedrome**. By 1922 with new owners the cinema showed one performance nightly and a matinee each Wednesday and Saturday. With the introduction of sound it seems that the owners were not prepared to invest in the new technology and the cinema closed 1931.

The **County Theatre**, Dean Street was originally the Tabernacle Chapel built 1850. In 1912 it was converted to a theatre with a stage and a fly tower built on one side. A balcony was added and the theatre could accommodate about 840 people. The theatre had a proscenium width of 30 feet with a stage depth of 40 feet and six dressing rooms at the rear. During the silent film era the County showed one nightly performance and a matinee every Wednesday and Saturday with a programme change twice a week. With the

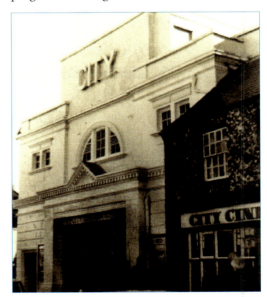

City Picture House, High Street, Bangor as a cinema (via Gwynedd Archives)

advent of the talkies in the early thirties the cinema installed the Western Electric Sound system which was regarded the best on the market at the time. During World War Two the theatre was taken over by the BBC when most of the organisation moved out of London. In 1944 the theatre/cinema was taken over by Leslie Blonde Organisation who owned a small cinema circuit and was registered as Bangor County Theatre and Cinema Company. The cinema reopened in February 1945. In 1956 Cinemascope system was installed and the seating was reduced to 800 seats to provide a better viewing for the patrons. The County continued to show films right up to 1971, together with the occasional live performance. After a brief period of closure it was refurbished and used for bingo and a social club. Just as the cinema attendance decline so too bingo and the building became empty once more until 1990 when it became various night clubs called the Bliss, Peep and the Octagon.

City Entertainments, Bangor in 2014

In 1919 the **New City Picture House** on the High Street was opened by Mr J R Saronie who at the time was involved in cinemas in Prestatyn. The New City Picture House built on a vacant site had a seating capacity of nearly 900. In the 1920s it was managed by a number of different managers on behalf of Mr Saronie. With the introduction of sound on film in the early thirties a brand new RCA reproducing system was installed. For most of the war year's film shows ceased but an occasional newsreel was shown. In 1945 the City Picture House was taken over by the Paramount Picture Theatre

Ltd. Under the new ownership minor refurbishment was completed including reducing the seating capacity to 569 seats. By now it was simply known as the City. Cinemascope was installed in 1956. The cinema continued to show films every night with matinees on Saturdays. In 1960 further improvements were made including an opening of a snack bar. With the death of Mr Guy Baker, Managing Director of Paramount Picture Theatres several of the cinemas were disposed of including the City in 1984. Fortunately the building has remained and has been converted into a snooker hall – City Leisure Amusements.

The **Plaza** was the only cinema that survived the downturn in attendances. The 1,084 seat cinema opened its doors in August 1934. Built on High Street more or less on the site of the Arcadia was the largest cinema in the city. It was equipped with the latest RCA Photophone sound system. In the 1950s the Plaza became under the control of Paramount Picture Theatres Ltd. With the introduction of Cinemascope seating capacity was reduced to 960 providing clear new line of sight for its patrons. The Hutchinson Leisure Ltd acquired the Plaza from Paramount and obtained a bingo licence. It was twined with the balcony converted to two cinemas – 310 and 198 seats, while the stalls were converted for bingo. In 1980 the cinema was taken over by the Apollo Leisure Group. A major refit took place in 1992 with the fitting of new lighting, a new curtains and carpets and installing Dolby stereo system. By the nineties the bingo hall had closed and Apollo put forward plans to convert the stalls to another screen, but when plans were approved to build a multiplex at Llandudno Junction the Plaza plan was dropped. In 2002 both screens and entrance hall was refurbished once again. In 2005 the cinema was taken over by an independent operator who kept it going for another year, but sadly it closed on 31st August 2006. Today a student accommodation has been built on the site.

The other place of entertainment at Bangor was on the University Campus was **Theatr Gwynedd** on Deiniol Road opened 1st January 1974. At the time it was the

1. County Theatre/Cinema, Bangor; 2. The County Theatre Octagon Night Club in 2015; 3. Auditorium of the County Theatre Bangor

most modern arts centre in the area. The dual purpose theatre had seating capacity of 340 seats. The projection box was equipped with both 35 mm and 16 mm projectors. Films were showed on one week per month while the rest of the month was devoted to live performances. In 2002 the theatre was refurbished and in 2006 was taken over, but it continued to lose money. The theatre finally closed in November 2008 because of inadequate funding problems and was demolished 2009/10. On the site a new arts centre, **Pontio**, has been built which is part of Bangor University. It consists of a 450 seat theatre and a 120 seat cinema with modern 3D digital projectors. The £49 million venue was opened in 2015 and is available to the general public.

At the time of writing plans were proposed for a new multiplex cinema on an industrial park on the outskirts of the town.

1. Theatr Gwynedd prior to demolition; 2. The Pontio, Bangor lavish auditorium; 3. The Plaza cinema was Bangor's premier cinema until its closure; 4. Today student's accommodation has been built on the cinema's site

6. Beaumaris, Anglesey

Beaumaris is famous for its 13th century castle, its elaborate gaol and the flying boat factory on the outskirts of the town. It only had one cinema the **Regal**, although films were shown by a local businessman around 1929/30. This gave rise to a 340 seat cinema equipped with Marshall Sound and projection system. In 1940 it was taken over by the Paramount Circuit which continued to show films throughout the war especially to the workers that were brought in to work at the Saunders Roe factory. In 1949 the projection equipment was upgrade by installing Kalee 11s or 12s. In 1955 it was upgrade once again to show Cinemascope picture but it did not make much different as the cinema closed in early 1960s. By today the building has been demolished and made way for a housing development.

The Regal Cinema, Beaumaris (via Cinema Treasure)

7. Benllech, Anglesey

The small town of Bellech is situated on the north western coast of Anglesey. Over the years the village has grown to be the fifth largest town on the island. Today it is a popular beach holiday destination.

The **Benllech Cinema** located in the Community Ex-Servicemen Hall.

The hall had seating capacity for approx. 300 people. The cinema operated during the summer months in the 1970s by a Mr D R Sutcliffe using 16mm projectors.

1. Kalee 11s became the standard projectors in the post war period, but were replaced by newer Kalees and other makes (National Media Museum); 2. A typical projector box in most cinemas in the thirties. This was at the Odeon Colwyn Bay. (via English Heritage)

8. Bethesda, Gwynedd

Bethesda is located on the edge of the Snowdonia and derived its name from a chapel. The town quickly grew as the result of the slate and stone quarries in the vicinity.

First film shows in the town was given by visiting Bioscope touring companies in the early part of the 1900s.

Public Hall Cinema began in 1920, with the advent of sound Uniquaphone sound system was installed in 1935. The cinema was run by a Mr C S Wakeham until the early thirties when the proprietor was listed as a Mr E H Jones who continued running the cinema until early fifties. Films were shown nightly Monday to Saturday with two film changes per week. Initially seating capacity was 500 but was reduced over the years. The cinema's proscenium width was 25 feet with a decent size stage which was used for live performances.

When the Public Hall ceased showing films a new cinema was built for Mr C W Beretta, the **Ogwen Cinema**. The cinema had seating capacity was 544. The proscenium width was 28 feet with a stage depth of 15 feet and two dressing rooms. In 1954 BTH projectors and sound system was installed but performances were reduced to one show Monday, Friday and Saturday. Cinemascope was installed in 1956 which gave a screen size of 26 feet wide. In the 1960s the Ogwen was taken over by Messrs W Richards and H Griffiths, but ceased showing films in 1970.

The Ogwen cinema was refurbished in 1988 and reopened as **Community/Cultural Centre** mostly used for live performances. However in 1990 due to public demand films were shown one night per week, the first being the war film 'Memphis Belle'. By mid-1991 film showing had ceased because of poor attendance. After further refurbishment it was renamed Neuadd Ogwen which opened in August 2014.

Ogwen Cinema, Bethesda

9. Betws-y-coed, Conwy

Betws-y-coed is situated in the Snowdonia National Park near where the River Conway is joined by two other rivers. By today it has become a centre for walkers.

Memorial Hall was built in 1927 in memory of those who died in the First World War had seating capacity for some 200 people and had an inbuilt projection box. It began showing films in the 1940s when E H James, Llanrwst Cinema Company ran it as a cinema. The arrangement continued until 1951 when it ceased to be a cinema. In the 1950 the Memorial Hall was listed as being equipped with BTH equipment. In the eighties the hall was refurbished and renamed **Nant y Nos** and 16mm projectors were installed replacing the 35mm equipment. The service was provided by theatre Theatr Gwynedd Film Service. In September 2000 the Reel Institute was formed and regularly showed one film per month, but in 2008 they were asked to vacate the premises.

Memorial Hall, Betws y Coed has been used as a cinema over the years

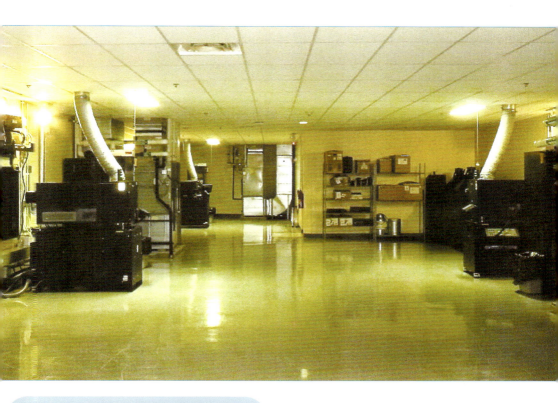

A modern multiplex projection box equipped with Digital projectors (via Cineworld)

10. Blaenau Ffestiniog

The town grew in size as the result of the slate industry; thousands of people move in to work in the quarries. The first recorded cinema was in 1913 when films were shown in the Gramophone Hall by a Mr G R Davies. The name was changed to **Assembly Rooms Cinema** and continued to show one performance per night.

The other cinema was the **Empire** on the High Street which was originally the Co-op Hall which began around 1925 showing two performances per night and three on Saturday. Programmes usually changed on Monday, Wednesday and Fridays. The 400 seat, Empire was quite profitable as in 1938 it registered as a new company called Blaenau Ffestiniog (Empire) Ltd with at least £2,000 in £1 shares. The cinema celebrated its 75th anniversary in 1986 but closed soon afterwards. Today it is a furniture store however there are some local interests to reopen it again as a cinema.

Park Cinema built in the mid-thirties had a seating capacity for 368 with a proscenium of 21 feet and was fitted with British Acoustic sound equipment but later changed to the latest BTH projectors and sound system. The building was a shed type structure with a shop type entrance. In 1935 a Mr W O Thomas was listed as the proprietor. There was a daily performance with film changes twice a week. The cinema closed in the late 1950s and was demolished making way for a housing development.

The Forum cinema in Market Place was opened by Captain W E Pritchard in January 1935. It was a 638 seat cinema with RCA projectors and sound system. By the outbreak of the war the Forum was run by a Manchester based Hoylake Entertainments Ltd. Film booking were conducted by Mr Jacobs at Rhyl. Cinemascope apparatus were fitted in 1956. The cinema continued to show films up to its closure in 1970. It was converted into a supermarket until it closed and the building was demolished in 1989.

The **Cell B Centre** formerly the Magistrate Court Building on the High Street has been converted into a

1. Park Cinema, Blaenau opened in the 1930s;
2. The Empire Cinema on the High Street (via Nat Museum of Wales);
3. The Empire building as it is today

community centre for the town. The venue includes a café-bar, hostel and a luxury cinema with digital projector capable of showing the latest releases and live shows from London and elsewhere.

1. *The Forum Cinema Market Place Blaenau opened in 1935 (via Cinema Treasure);*
2. *The town newest venue is Cell B, located at the old police station*

11. Broughton, Flintshire

The village is most famous for its airfield and the aircraft factory nearby. The earliest account of a cinema was in the early 1920s but the location of the venue is unknown.

Since then the area including Hawarden has grown with new homes and shopping parks. On 8th May 2015 a new cinema complex – **Cineworld** opened on Broughton Shopping Park. The 11 screen multiplex has total seating for 1,680. The cinema boasts of the most comfortable layout in North Wales as well as having the first 70 x 9 metre **IMAX** screen in the area. All the cinemas are equipped with 4k digital projectors.

1. Cineworld multiplex, Broughton is the only IMAX cinema in North Wales;
2. Promotion Card for the new Cineworld Multiplex (Broughton Promotions)

12. Brymbo, near Wrexham

A small village to the north west of Wrexham became prominent during the 1900s because of coal and iron production in the vicinity.

Film showing was introduced into the village in the 1900s with visiting Myriorama (moving pictures) with trumpet speaking machine and also in the 1920s by visiting film showmen.

The first purposely built cinema was located on Railway Road near the Queens Head public house. Built in 1930 by the Grainger family but was first listed in Kinematograph Year Book with a Mr A Davies as manager. Morrison sound equipment was fitted from the beginning. It continued to operate throughout the Second World War, even when the nearby steel works was bombed in August 1940 and the Queens Head was hit it the cinema carried on showing 'Tell no Tales' starring Melvyn Douglas and 'Ice Follies of 1939' starring Joan Crawford and James Stewart. It was last listed as a cinema in 1966 and was later utilised as Valley Hall. Eventually it closed and the projection room, the façade and other sections was demolished. Today it is Queens Cross Garage.

13. Buckley, Flintshire

Like most of the small towns and villages in North Wales the earliest cinemas or more appropriate film shows and exhibitions were brought by travelling showmen either in fairs or at any public halls.

The Buckley Picture House Ltd was formed and registered on 28th January 1913 with a working capital of £8,000. The directors being Messrs F Barnett, H Firms, JD Walsh, G W Greenwood and J S Hayes. The **Palace Picture House** was a 400 seat cinema but the building included a billiard hall, a printing hall and a post office. In the 1920s the cinema assets were taken over by Messrs Cropper and Son and Mr T N Cropper became the manager. Initially the cinema showed only one performance nightly with a matinee on Saturdays. With the introduction of the talkies in 1930 the cinema installed British Acoustic sound system.

1. Bethesda's Public Hall auditorium in the 1920s (via Welsh Cinema History);
2. Tivoli cinema, Buckley (R Sloane);
3. The Tivoli cinema was converted into the Tivoli Night Club (via Daily Post)

When Cinemascope was installed in 1956 the ownership had been transferred to a Mr J Robinson. The cinema layout changed considerably with the installation of a wide screen. The normal 14 feet screen had to be extended to 18 feet, the proscenium was only 19 feet. In the 1960 the cinema was licensed to hold 331 people but was soon taken over by Wedgewood Cinemas of Colwyn Bay who after conducting a survey found that it needed extensive structural work. The cinema closed and was later demolished in 1975.

The **Central Hall**, Brunswick Road built in 1894 was used to show silent films before the Palace was built. However the hall was demolished in the twenties and the Tivoli was built on the site.

The **Tivoli** was a purposely built cinema/theatre it had 30 feet deep stage and a 38 feet proscenium arch sufficient to put on the most lavish stage productions. There were 6 decent size changing rooms for the artists. The 980 seat theatre was opened in 1925 and with the advent of the talkies a Filmophone sound system was installed. The Tivoli together with the Alhambra at Shotton was taken over by Stanley Grimshaw Theatres then by Byrom Pictures and later by Philip Hanmer of Liverpool.

In late 1940s the cinema was listed as having the largest wide screen in the area a 30 feet x 22 feet. With the installation of Cinemascope in the mid-1950s the screen width extended to 37 feet wide.

As with most cinema attendances declined and the Tivoli stopped showing films and converted to bingo. In turn live bingo declined also and the building was turned to a night club called the Trend but reverted to the old name Tivoli. Recently the Tivoli has been in the news as a haunted theatre.

14. Caergwrle, Flintshire

A small town within the colliery area of Flint and Denbigh is more famous for its 13th century castle than its cinema.

It was built by the landlord of the Derby Inn in 1919 and opened in 1920. The cinema was named after the inn – the **Derby Cinema**, although it was referred as the Derry in Kinematograph Year Books. The unusual white painted structure with black painted wooden frame is very similar to a Tudor building and is visible for miles. Initially the cinema was run by the Rural Cinema Company later by the Wrexham based Cambria and Border Cinemas. The 300 seat cinema had a 22 foot proscenium and in the thirties was equipped with the Cambriaphone sound system. After the Second World War ownership of the cinema passed to Mr J Jervis of Buckley who re-equipped the well-attended cinema with Kalee projectors and sound system in the fifties. Cinemascope was introduced to the Derby in 1954. The last owner of the cinema was Mr Croley from Brecon before it closed around 1963 because of lack of support. Today the building still stands on Castle Street and it's used as an industrial premises.

1 *The Derby Cinema in the 1940s (Silver Screen Archives); 2. The Derby Cinema, Caergwrle was built in the 1920s; 3. The Derby building today is used by a local firm; 4. Empire Cinema, Caernarfon was converted to Bingo; 5. The Empire cinema on Crown Street today*

15. Caernarfon, Gwynedd

The town of Caernarfon is more famous for its 13th century castles rather than its places of entertainment.

The town's first encounter with moving pictures was early 1900s when various traveling film showmen visited the area with their Bioscope shows.

The **Guildhall** was perhaps the first cinema in the town dated around 1910, called the New Hall and was ran by the film maker Wilf Onda (real name Hugh Rains). The building was owned by the Borough Corporation which was capable of holding 450 people and according to some sources held Saturday afternoon's matinee. In 1913 it was fitted with the synchronised gramophone sound system. The sound system was modernised in the 1930s with the installation of the British Acoustic system. During the 1939-45 war the cinema was ran by a Mr RA Davies and ran a continuous film show with matinees on Wednesday and Saturdays. In 1948 the lease holder was Mr A Jacobs who introduced three film changes each week. Eventually, Paramount Picture Theatres Ltd took over control of the cinema, but in 1960 relinquished the lease and the cinema was closed. Paramount had already taken over the Empire and Majestic cinemas in the town.

Caernarfon's other cinema mentioned during the same period was the **Pavilion Cinema** just off Bangor Street. The Pavilion was built in 1877 and was capable of holding 8,000 people. Over the next few years it often held opening ceremonies for the National Eisteddfod of Wales, as well as large religious and political gatherings. The Pavilion was 200 feet x 100 feet with a large stage with a skating rink in front. It was first mentioned as being a cinema in 1914. Films were shown on particular days or special film events. By the 1930s other cinemas had opened in the town and all film showing in the Pavilion ceased. During the war the building was requisitioned and used by the military. After the war the upkeep of the Pavilion was extremely high and was eventually demolished in 1961.

The **Empire** in Crown Street was the first purposely built cinema which opened

1. Majestic Cinema on Bangor Road in its heyday in the sixties; 2. The Majestic Caernarfon as it was in 2014

The Galeri Centre is a theatre/Cinema complex

in 1915 as the **Empire Picture Palace**. The Playhouse (Caernarfon) Ltd ran the cinema after the war with Mr Caradoc Rowlands as manager. The 500 seat cinema showed one performance nightly with two on the Saturday, there was a programme change twice a week. In the 1930s the new owners Caernarvon Cinema Company Ltd installed the British Acoustic sound system. The number of performances remained the same throughout the thirties except there were three shows given on a Saturday. The cinema ownership changed once again in late 1930s but the building was eventually taken over by Paramount Theatres in 1940. Cinemascope was installed in 1956 which meant that the seating had to be reduced to 478. The Empire was equipped with Kalee 12s with Peerless Carbon Arcs and a Western Electric sound system.

With cinema attendances' declining the Empire was granted a bingo licence in 1970 and films were only shown four nights a week, but within ten years films were discontinued. In 1986 the building was totally refurbished as a bingo hall.

The **Majestic Cinema** on Bangor Road opened in August 1934 with Jessie Matthews in the film 'Evergreen'. The cinema was built for Captain W E Pritchard and his partner Mr E H Jonathan and had a seating capacity of 1,050. The proscenium was 26 feet in width and a screen of some 18 x 11 feet. The super cinema as it was known had also a café for its patrons. It was equipped with Kalee12s with Peerless carbon arcs and the sound system was by Western Electric. A new company was registered in January 1945 as Majestic Cinema (Caernarvon) Ltd but the real owners were Paramount Theatres of Welshpool. Cinemascope was introduced in mid-fifties. Occasional concerts and a monthly wrestling event were held at the venue. The cinema closed in 1980 and converted to the Majestic Entertainment Centre, then to Northern Leisure Nightclub and eventually renamed the Dome Nightclub. However on the 16th January 1994 the building was gutted by a fire as a result of an arson attack.

A new arts centre was built in Victoria Docks called the **Galeri** which is a 394 seat theatre/ cinema venue. Live performances are given as well as film shows. At the time of writing a two screen cinema extension is in the process of being built comprising of a 119 seat and 71 seat cinemas.

16. Caerwys, Flintshire

A small town with a lot of history and was first mentioned in the Domesday Book.

Town Hall Cinema showed silent films regularly between 1913 and 1920 but closed as a cinema 1926. The cinema was run by the Bullen and Broome Film Company showing three nights per week, sometimes with an accompanied piano player.

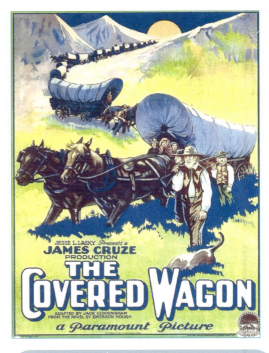

Poster for Covered Wagon shown at Stanley's Kinema, Cefn Mawr

17. Cefn Mawr, Wrexham

Cefn Mawr is a large village on the outskirts of Wrexham and south of Ruabon. It rose to prominence because of the heavy industry of the 18th and 19th centuries.

Memorial Hall, Well Street was often referred to as the **People's Cinema** and **Stanley's Cinema**. The hall had a seating capacity for 600 people and had proscenium of 26 feet and a stage depth of 18 feet. According to Kinematograph Year Book for 1924 there were two shows daily at 6pm and 8pm with a matinee on a Wednesday at 3 o'clock. The venue was originally equipped with AWH sound system but later changed to British Acoustic sound system. The hall is still used for various events and today it is known as George Edwards Memorial Hall.

Also there was the **Palace**, a 700 seat cinema on Hill Street. Initially it was equipped with British Acoustic sound system but by 1950 had converted to RCA sound system. The Palace showed continuous performance for most of the time and remained opened throughout the war years. In 1950 the cinema proprietor was listed as Mr A Jacobs and the seating had been reduced to 550 seats. Like most local cinemas in the fifties it eventually closed.

1. The Memorial Hall, Well Street, Cefn Mawr was used as a cinema; 2. Today it is known as the George Edwards Hall

18. Chirk, Wrexham

Chirk today is re-known for its nearby canal aqueduct next to the railway viaduct across the valley

Parish Hall, the Wharf ran films by visiting companies in 1921 with four shows per week and usually two changes each week. In 1928 it was run by the Cambrian and Border Cinema Company of Wrexham. According to 1934 Kinematograph Year Book the cinema was registered to Chirk Empire Cinema and was renamed Empire Electric cinema .The 450 seat cinema was equipped with Gyrotone sound system and had a stage some 10 feet in depth and two dressing rooms. In March 1936 the hall was leased to Mr W E Jones of Corwen. It continued to show films throughout the war years but closed in 1946 with the venue reverting back to a Parish Hall status.

The Cinema, Temple Row was also listed as a cinema in Kinematograph Year Book of 1925.

19. Coedpoeth

Coedpoeth is an industrial village on the outskirts of the town of Wrexham.

Currah's Myriorama (moving picture) plus gramophone and trumpet speaking machine was advertised appearing in the village in 1901.

In the Kinematograph Year Book for 1914 there was listed the **Cinema** on Park Road showing two performances per week. It is certain the venue used was the Parish Hall. It seems the cinema changed its name to the **Regent** in the 1920s when it was taken over by the Cambria and Border Cinemas Ltd. With the advent of sound Western Electric system was installed in 1930. Because of its closeness to Wrexham it is believed the cinema closed in around 1935.

20. Colwyn Bay, Conwy

A seaside town with its long promenade grew to prominence in the Victorian era. Today it's famous for the Welsh Mountain Zoo which overlooks the town.

Arthur Cheetham opened his first cinema in Colwyn Bay in 1908, followed by another in 1910 in a converted Welsh Methodist Chapel, 6 Conway Road, although it only remained in use until 1912. The screen was situated on the wall in between the entrances with the projector box situated on the three row balcony. The chapel's pews were used for seating.

In 1912/3 the local architect Sidney Colwyn Foulkes was asked to design a new cinema from the remnants of the old chapel incorporating some shops in front of the chapel.

Roadside entrance was through a passage between two shops, the screen remained between the two main entrances, but a brick extension was built at the rear of the building for the projector box. The pews were replaced by cinema seats and the hall was capable of holding 300 people. The proprietor Mr Watson Hartley who ran the cinema until it closed in September 1926. By now the cinema had become known as the **Cosy Cinema**. It was taken over by the Cambria and Border Cinemas and Brook Richards became the manager who reopened the cinema on 18th July 1927. Mr Richards an ex BBC entertainer, introduced the Cosy Orchestra under the direction of Mr H Tideswell to accompany the silent films and during the intermission. There was a continuous performance from 2.30 most days, Monday to Fridays. With the introduction of the talkies the Electrochord sound system was installed in the cinema in 1929 but later replaced by an improved system, the Western Electric sound system. In 1937 the cinema was taken over by Cosy Cinema (Colwyn Bay)

Cosy Cinema was closed in 1954 (via Colwyn Bay Library)

Ltd a company formed by M A Kenyon who also was the owner of the Princess Cinema. The new owner re-equipped the cinema with BTH projectors and sound system. By the early fifties the cinema had become uneconomical to run and rather than converting the cinema for Cinemascope, Mr Kenyon decided to close the Cosy in 1954 to concentrate on the Princess Cinema.

Another pioneer James Robert Saronie, Royal Biograph appeared at the Town Hall for two nights in November 1909. A favourite venue for these early showmen was the **Bijou Theatre** on the pier which opened around 1900. The Bijou had a reasonable size stage for live entertainment and could hold 600 people. The theatre concentrated more on live performances rather than film shows but the venue was available film screening if required. However it was destroyed by fire in 1922 and after a costly rebuild it was again destroyed by fire in July 1933.

In 1885 a new hall was built by the Public Hall Company for the benefit of the people of Colwyn Bay. The first ever film shows to take place was Shadowgraph shows conducted by Harry Reynolds during his Serenade Minstrel Troupe

Colwyn Bay other cinema was the Arcadia/ Wedgewood on Princes Drive (Silver Screen Archive)

variety show. By 1909 the hall had been converted into Colwyn Bay first picture house with electric light. Unrivalled Animated Pictures screened several short films on January 25 1909 which was perhaps the first performances ever. Mr Harry Reynolds who had ran the hall continued until 1922 when he sold the business to Mr Pittingale of Coastal Cinema Ltd who renamed it the **Rialto**. The hall could accommodate 800 people and the stage had a depth of 24 feet capable of putting on live shows. The venue closed in 1930 after a devastating roof fire which also caused severe damage in the auditorium. It was re-roofed and the auditorium repaired and re- decorated with a new stage and dressing rooms. Western Electric Sound was fitted and a new café was opened in the foyer as well as adopting a new name the **New Rialto**. A Repertory Theatre under the leadership of Stanley Ravenscroft was formed and stayed at the theatre for 22 years. During the Second World War the theatre was closed but after hostilities ceased, opened with summer shows and film shows during the winter months. In 1959 the building was bought by the council for £12,000 and became known as **The Prince of Wales**. As it was the only theatre in Colwyn Bay it continued to hold live shows. In 1991 it was renamed again to **Theatre Colwyn** and in 1996 the County Borough of Conway was formed and took over the running of the theatre.

With financial help from the Welsh Assembly Government and Conwy Council, the £740,000 refurbishment was completed in September 2011 and was reopened on 16th October. The venue shows up-to-date films live performances and live broadcast of shows, opera, ballet from London theatre land.

The traditional 35mm projectors were

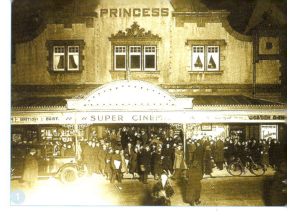

1. Princess Cinema on Princes Drive opened in October 1922; 2. The Princess before alteration of the frontage we see today

replaced with a Sony 4k digital projector.

William Catlin's Royal Perrott's performed regularly in a wooden hall on Princes Drive. In 1918 a new 1,000 seat venue was built, designed by Sidney Colwyn Foulkes. The **Arcadia** as it was known opened in 1920. In 1929 a Fitton and Haley concert organ was fitted to accompany both variety shows and silent films. Two years later with the coming of talkies a Western Electric sound system was installed. In the early thirties the venue was advertised as **Catlin's Arcadia Winter Gardens and Picture House**. The theatre proscenium was some 30 feet wide mostly to take advantage of Catlin's live shows. When cinema was re- introduced in late 1955 it had a 26 foot screen. In 1967 the cinema was taken over by J Daigliesh's Wedgewood Cinemas Ltd and was renamed **Wedgewood Cinema**. For most of its time the cinema showed continuous performances. The Wedgewood closed in February 1979 with the showing of the film 'Grease'. For many years the cinema frontage was used as a garage although the auditorium and stage area was demolished in the 1980s during the building of the A55 dual carriage way. Today the garage has been demolished and the Royal Mail sorting office has been built on the site.

By today only the **Princess Cinema** building remains standing and more or less untacked. The Princess on Princes Drive in view of the Arcadia was built for Messrs Kington and Jeffrey. The super cinema as it was referred to opened in October 1922 with Jackie Coogan's film 'The Kid' (1921) which attracted a large crowd and was followed by the film 'A Tale of Two Worlds' (1921).

There were two shows daily with a matinee twice a week and usually a change of films twice a week. Initially it was a single floor auditorium. In 1932 a balcony was added increasing the seating capacity to 800. Also a new façade was added in the Neo-Egyptian style. In December 1937 the cinema closed for renovations, and re-opened again with the film 'A Day at the Races' (1937). The cinema was equipped with BTH projectors and sound system. It had a 32 foot proscenium and a 30 foot stage capable of hosting a live performance. By now M A Kenyon and Son was registered as owners. The Princess continued to show films throughout the

1. The interior converted into a bingo club (via J D Wethertspoon); 2. The Princess was taken over by Wetherspoon Pubs which have kept the foyer as it was; 3. Prince of Wales theatre (Theatre Colwyn) is the town oldest venue (Courtesy Theatr Colwyn); 4. The theatre was renamed Theatr Colwyn

war years. Cinemascope was introduced in 1954/5 with a 20 foot screen but the seating was reduced to 645 seats. The Hutchinson Leisure Group took over control of the Princess in 1970, but the group itself was taken over by Apollo Leisure (UK) Ltd. Cinema attendance fell and in 1981 the cinema closed and was converted to bingo. In 1989 Apollo proposed to make the balcony a cinema while utilising the stalls area for bingo but the plan never materialised. The Princess continued to operate as a bingo club until 30th August 1997 when it closed for good. It was acquired by Wetherspoon and opened as a pub in September 1998 called the Picture House. The company utilised the large foyer area as the pub with just minor alterations. The auditorium remained the same but closed off.

Colwyn Bay fourth cinema was the largest and most lavish of the venues in the town, the **Odeon** on Conway Road which was built in 1934 at the cost of £13,000. The cinema designed by J Cecil Clavering was very similar to other Odeon's in the country. It had a narrow tower covered in cream tiles with the word Odeon written on the side. There were 1,128 seats in the stalls and 578 in the balcony. The walls was plain except for vertical bars on either side of the stage covering the ventilation grills, it had a small stage and few dressing rooms at the rear but were never used. The Odeon was equipped with 1930 series BTH projectors and sound system. Colwyn Bay's Odeon cinema was opened on Saturday 25th April 1936 with Robert Donat's film 'The Ghost Goes West' (1935). The cinema remained opened throughout the Second World War. Cinemascope was installed in 1954. During the fifties a number of Odeon Cinemas closed throughout the country and on 5th January 1957 Colwyn Bay Odeon showed its last film, Michael Craig in 'The House of Secrets' (1956). The building lay derelict for ten years until it was leased to the Hutchinson Leisure Group who reopened the cinema as **Astra Entertainment Centre** on 8th June 1966. The balcony remained as a cinema while the stalls area was converted as a bingo hall. With a decline in both cinema and bingo attendances, the bingo hall closed in March 1986 and the cinema closed on 10th October in the same year. As there was no other alternative use for the building it was demolished in 1987 and an apartment block was built on the site.

1. The Odeon cinema Colwyn Bay was taken over by the Hutchinson Group and re-named the Astra in 1967; 2. The Astra Cinema, Conway Road in its heyday

21. Connah's Quay, Flintshire

The **Hippodrome** cinema on the High Street was built by Arthur Correlli in 1910 but its ownership changed after World War 1. The cinema showed one performance nightly (Monday-Friday) and two on a Saturday. With the advent of sound and new owners, Enterprise Cinema Company Ltd, British Acoustic system was fitted. In 1935 the cinema was modernised, with new ventilation and heating, new seating, an Art Deco brick façade. The projection box was also refurbished. The 700 seat auditorium had a proscenium of 27 feet wide and a screen of 16 x 12 feet. In 1949 the Hippodrome was equipped with the Imperial sound system. The Hippodrome showed its last film in May 1962 with Deborah Kerr in 'The Innocents'. For the rest of the decade it was converted to a bingo hall but now it's a second hand furniture store.

In 2010 a new Community Cinema was set up at Connah's Quay Civic Hall.

The Hippodrome Cinema on the High Street in 1915 (Angeline.Com)

The film the Innocents was the last film shown at the Hippodrome May 1962

22. Conwy, Conwy

Conwy, a popular tourist destination is famous its castle and exquisite town walls.

The town first cinema dates back to pre-World War One with a 250 seat building on Bangor Road. Details of the cinema are very sketchy and there is no reference in any of the county's archive. It is believed it could be a mobile canvas covered tent as was common used by the travelling showmen in fairs.

The first true cinema recorded in Conway was the Town Hall (the **Town Cinema**) a room situated on the second floor and could hold 750 people. Throughout the war it continued to show mostly war newsreel films on ad hoc basis. In the 1920s the shows was controlled by Edward Pittingale who was the General Manager of Coast Cinemas Ltd.

There was a nightly film performances Monday to Friday with an occasional matinee and usually three programme changes during the week. The hall was equipped with a stage of about 18 feet deep and 24 feet wide with at least four dressing rooms was available when live performances took place. Projectors and sound system operated in the 1930s were the Kamm equipment. By now the cinema was referred to as the Assembly Rooms but in 1930 license was withdrawn as the building did not conform to the fire regulation in accordance with the Cinematograph Act, however after minor improvements and alterations it was allowed to continue but closed in 1938. **The Assembly Hall** completely closed to the public again in 1961 but in May 1966 the whole building caught fire and was totally destroyed. The hall was rebuilt but it's only used for live performances.

On 6th January 1937 the **Palace Cinema** on the High Street opened its door for the first time with the showing of a film starring Hugh Williams called 'Lieutenant Daring RN' (1935). The 750 seat auditorium was designed by the architect Sidney Colwyn Foulkes and built of local stone. It was equipped with Western Electric projectors and sound system and the cinema was lit by special lightning fitted by the Holophone Company, which automatically changed colours. The proscenium arch was 28 feet with a small stage and two dressing rooms. There was a balcony with a café in the foyer. The owner was Mr H Christian Jones but by 1940 the cinema was ran by his wife Mrs Florence Jones.

With the introduction of Cinemascope in the fifties the 27 foot screen filled nearly all the stage area. Performances were continuous starting at 5.30 pm each evening. Utilising the stage several live concerts was held at the cinema during the early 1980s. By now the cinema had been taken over by the Parker's Leisure Holdings Ltd who introduced bingo to the Palace. Film attendance dropped and in 1995 film showing ceased altogether concentrating on bingo. The stall area was completely converted as a bingo hall and social club with a restaurant on the balcony foyer. The bingo hall finally closed its door in 2013. As it is a Listed II building several proposals have been put forward including an interest from Wetherspoon Pubs Ltd.

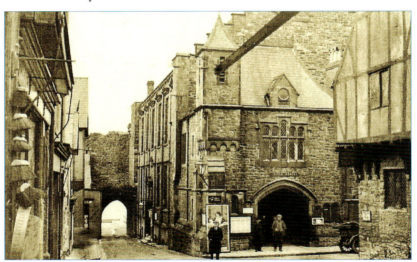

The Civic Hall was one of Conwy's earliest cinemas

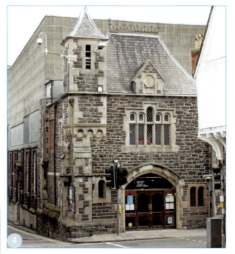

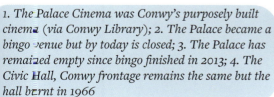

1. The Palace Cinema was Conwy's purposely built cinema (via Conwy Library); 2. The Palace became a bingo venue but by today is closed; 3. The Palace has remained empty since bingo finished in 2013; 4. The Civic Hall, Conwy frontage remains the same but the hall burnt in 1966

23. Corwen, Denbighshire

Corwen a small town on the A5 road had one cinema, a 394 seat auditorium built in the late thirties. Prior to that occasional film show was held in the church house. The **Glyndŵr Cinema** on Green Lane was equipped for the talkies from the start with a Gyrotone system and Kalee projectors. It had a proscenium of 28 feet sufficient to show Cinemascope films in the fifties. In 1945 the cinema became under the control of the Paramount Cinema Circuit and performances were only given certain nights per week. By the 1980 there were only limited shows during the summer months and with the decline in cinema attendances it closed by the end of the decade. Initially it became a supermarket but by today it's a DIY store.

The Glyndwr cinema Corwen closed in the seventies

The cinema today is used by a DIY retailer

24. Cricieth, Gwynedd

Cricieth a delightful sea side resort with its castle overlooking town and sea shore had one cinema/theatre the **Memorial Hall** on the High Street. The hall was erected in memory of those died in the First World War and was formally opened in 1925. It was first recorded as a cinema in 1929 with a seating capacity for up to 600 people and equipped with Kalee projectors and British Acoustic sound system. Seating was removable and the ground floor was often used for dancing. In 1937s one performance nightly was given during the summer months with two performances off season. This arrangement remained more or less until it ceased showing films around 1966. The theatre had a small stage with a 28 foot proscenium. Dressing rooms were situated to the side and rear of the building. In 1945 the cinema came under the control of Paramount Theatres and operated as Cricieth Cinema Ltd. Post war the sound system was changed to AWH and Cinemascope was introduced, but as the proscenium was rather small it seems the screen size was restricted. By 1980 all film showing had ceased and today the building is used for theatre productions and community events.

The Memorial Hall, Cricieth have been showing films since 1929

The Memorial Hall auditorium

25. Denbigh, Denbighshire

The market town with its castle overlooks the Vale of Clwyd.

The first cinema recorded in this county town was the **Picture House** on Market Street which opened in November 1913. The converted hall had a seating capacity of 500 in tip-up seats. It was renamed the **Picturedrome** by the time it was taken over by Bullen and Broome Film Company in 1922. Three different shows weekly were given. In 1924 a Mr J F Broome was registered as the proprietor and manager who is reported reduced the admission charges as the result of high unemployment in the area. By the thirties and the introduction of sound the cinema had been taken over by the Enterprise Cinema Company but for some unknown reasons it closed in 1936.

The other cinema in Denbigh was the **Scala**, on Love Lane which opened in 1929 equipped with sound system by British Acoustic and was run by the Denbigh Scala Ltd. The cinema had 450 seats, the proscenium was rather small just 20 feet wide and the screen was only 14 x 10 feet. The Scala continued to show films throughout the Second World War. In 1948 films were shown twice nightly with matinees on Mondays, Thursdays and Saturdays. Cinemascope was installed in 1956 but the small width of the screen was only increased slightly. In 1963 the cinema was taken over by Wedgewood Cinemas of Colwyn Bay who refurbished the auditorium and installed BTH projectors and sound system, renaming it the **Wedgewood**. Seating had been reduced to 212 seats when Mr S Horowitz leased the cinema in the seventies. The state of the structure caused great concern as the roof leaked and the walls had damp rot. So the cinema closed on 26th October 1980 with two horror films 'Rabid' and 'The Dead of Night'. In 1981 it was taken over by a Mr Peter Moore who did extensive repair to the property and opened it in January 1982 as the **Futura** cinema. Structural problems continued to haunt the cinema, but remained opened until 1st April 1996, especially after Peter Moore was convicted of murder and jailed for life. For a brief period the cinema was used as a second hand furniture store, and then became empty and eventually demolished. Today apartments have been built on the site.

1. *Futura Cinema, Love Lane, Denbigh opened in 1929 as the Scala Cinema (Courtesy of Denbigh Archives); 2. The cinema closed in the early nineties and became derelict; 3. Today modern apartments have been built on the site.*

26. Flint, Flintshire

Another of North Wales town famous for its castle and industrial heritage.

Flint originally had three cinemas, two of which has been demolished. The first to be built was the **Empire Picture Hall** in 1912; it was a 500 seat cinema built with a steel frame and wooden and corrugated iron side walls and roof. In the early 1920s it was taken over by a Mr Robert Davis who changed its name to **Empire Cinema**. It advertised one film showing per evening and a programme change three times weekly. A pianist accompanied many films especially during the interval. Sound equipment was installed in 1930 with an AWH sound system. It continued to show films throughout the war years but by mid-fifties attendances had declined that the cinema was forced to close on 6th April 1957. The building was demolished in the 1960s.

The **Grand Cinema** in Church Road owned by Mr Robert Davis opened on 30th August 1920. The cinema was purposely built as a cinema/theatre with a 26 foot wide x 15 foot deep stage capable of holding live performances. There were two spacious dressing rooms at the rear of the building. Seating capacity was 900 but was reduced to 510 by the time it closed. The proscenium was 25 feet wide which gave a 22 foot wide Cinemascope screen that was installed in 1956/7. AWH sound system was installed in the 1930s but the system was replaced after the war. Films were changed twice a week, there were two shows on a Monday and Saturday with one showing Tuesday to Thursday; the cinema was closed on Fridays for live performances. Like so many other cinemas in North Wales in the 1960s the Grand attendances declined and the cinema closed in the mid-sixties and the building was demolished in 1968.

The third Flint cinema was the **Plaza** built by a new company the Flint Enterprise Cinemas Ltd which first registered in November 1937. The new cinema designed by a leading cinema architect Mr Sydney C Foulkes was built at the top of Church Street (no 96). The Plaza referred to as a super cinema had a seating capacity of 1,100 seats and was equipped with GB Kalee projectors and sound system. The auditorium was lit by Holophane lighting which changed colours

1. *The Grand Theatre/Cinema on Church Road, Flint; 2. Demolishing the Grand Theatre 1968 (Flint Archives); 3. The Empire Cinema dates back to pre-World War One (Flint Archives); 4. The Empire during demolition (Courtesy of Flint Archive)*

automatically. The proscenium was 35 feet in width with a small stage in front of the 20 x 15 foot screen. Surrounding the proscenium were panels painted with signs of the zodiac. The cinema opened on the 26th December 1938 with a Gracie Fields film 'We're Going to Be Rich'. When cinemascope was installed in 1956 the screen size was increased to 32 feet wide, the largest cinema screen in North Wales. In 1967 the Plaza was sold to Wedgewood Cinemas of Colwyn Bay and renamed the **Wedgewood Cinema**. After refurbishment it re-opened on Boxing Day 1967. Wedgewood sold the cinema to Mecca Ltd in 1974/5 who continued to run it as a bingo/ cinema concern but showed its last film 'Godspell' on 1st August 1975. It remained a bingo hall until it closed in 2011. Eventually the Plaza was put up for sale and was acquired with views of converting it to a cinema once more. In 2016 Mr Ashley Whyatt who ran several cinemas in Kent and Essex took over the running of the Plaza, renaming it Gaumont Plaza. The stalls have been converted to Screen 1 with 140 seats with future plans to convert the balcony to two 50 seat screens. Date of opening was 10th December 2016.

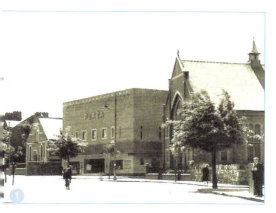

1. *Flint Plaza Cinema was a 1,100 seat cinema (via Flint Archives)*; 2. *The Plaza was turned into a bingo hall*; 3. *The auditorium during its bingo days (via Mecca Bingo)*; 4. *In 2015 the Plaza was acquired as a cinema and renamed the Plaza Gaumont (via Plaza Gaumont)*

27. Hawarden, Flintshire

Films were shown in the **Town Hall** in 1921 by Messrs Bullen and Broome Film Company, a visiting company that served a number of outlying areas. The manager was listed as a Mr P J Cleefe. Silent films were shown three nights a week with a different film each night.

The Cybi Hall in Treaddur Sq. Holyhead was a multi-purpose entertainment centre (via Welsh Cinema History

The site of the Hippodrome Cinema is occupied by a supermarket. The Cinema frontage still remains

28. Holyhead, Anglesey

The seaport of Holyhead has been fortunate to have several cinemas over the years. The **Town Hall** on Newry Street was first recorded has a venue for film showing. The early 19th century brick built hall had a wide stage with a depth of 18 feet which was the town main venue for concerts. The 800 seat hall was licenced for film showing in 1910 shortly after Messrs Davies and McCormack took over the running of the cinema. The Davies family continued to run the venue until the cinema ceased in 1931. There were two performances each night Monday to Saturday with an occasional matinee on Saturday afternoon. The cinema mostly showed silent films until its closure as no sound system was ever permanently installed. However there are some reports that Vitaphone sound and disc was acquired especially for the showing of the 'Jazz Singer' (1927 version). The hall remained a venue for concerts but eventually closed and the building is up for sale.

Another venue utilised as a cinema was **Victoria Hall**, a Bioscope ran by Mr Rees-Davies. Evidence of the cinema is rather sketchy as it could have been used by a travelling cinema that toured the north Wales coast in the 1900s. Also Arthur Cheetham has been associated with the site as he spent some time in Holyhead filming ships in the port.

The **Hippodrome** in Market Street was originally built as a music hall. It had a proscenium of 17 feet with two dressing rooms. Towards the end of the First World War it began showing films. In the early twenties film showing was continuous throughout the week. The first sound equipment was the Mihaly but was replaced in the thirties by British Talking Pictures system. The Hippodrome continued to show films in the 1940s and was a popular venue with service men in the town. In 1954 the cinema was refurbished and the seating was reduced from 488 to 465 and eventually to 445. The proscenium was widened to 24 feet ready for Cinemascope installation in 1955. Film shows were continuous with one performance each night and a matinee on Saturday. The last film showed at the Hippodrome was Cliff Robertson in '633 Squadron' on 20th February 1965. The building remained empty for a few years but was badly damaged by fire in the late sixties. Eventually the building was rebuilt and became a supermarket.

Holyhead other cinema is the **Empire** in Stanley Road. Originally built as a music hall during the First World War but was only completed in 1918. According to early photos it had a large house frontage and a large building to the rear. It is believed it opened in early 1920s showing films with two shows nightly and a special matinee on a Saturday. The cinema had 735 seats and a proscenium of 30 feet in width. In 1928 the cinema was taken over by a new company the Holyhead Empire Theatre Company Ltd. and in 1930 with advent of the talkies RCA sound equipment was installed. Throughout the war years the Empire continued to show films. In the mid-fifties, cinemascope was installed which increased the screen size to 27 feet. A Mr Johnston was registered as the owner of the cinema and remained so well into the seventies. The Hutchinson Leisure Group took over the control of the Empire whom in the late eighties converted it to a twin. Screen 1 situated in the stalls became an amusement venue with bingo and Screen 2 in the balcony a cinema. The cinema due to poor attendances and loss of revenue closed in February 1992. It remained closed until taken over by Messrs Moore and Blakemore (Focus Cinemas) on 9th December 1994. It reopened with the films 'The Lion King' and 'Snow White and the Seven Dwarfs'. Sadly the venture came to an abrupt end a year later when Mr Moore was arrested and jailed for murder. After a period of closure it reopened for a brief period as a bingo hall. In 2012 it was decided to get finance from Europe to re-develop the site for the people of Holyhead. It closed in April 2013 and after spending nearly half a million pound on the scheme the new complex reopened on 20th November 2013. The down stairs seating was removed and the floor flattened, the projector box was removed to make way

1. *Empire/Regal Cinema, Stanley Road, Holyhead (via Welsh Cinema History); 2. The Empire was converted into a two screen cinema in the late eighties; 3. The cinema was transformed into a cinema/ bingo venue; 4. The Empire Holyhead today is a modern entertainment centre after a £250 thousand refurbishment*

for a play centre, a Laser Tag and a cafe. The cinema upstairs was re-seated with plush seating, new proscenium with new curtains and lighting. It was equipped with digital projectors and full stereo sound system.

Cybi Hall cinema in Treaddur Square dates back to the early thirties when it was used regularly by the travelling film showmen. The hall was converted as a 240 seat cinema by Messrs Johnston and Berretta in 1945/6. It had a 15 foot wide screen and was fitted with the Morrison sound system. In 1956 cinemascope equipment was installed with the screen width increasing to 18 feet but seating had to be reduced to about 200. Over the next few years the Cybi cinema had three different owners. Towards the end of the sixties it was only showing films on few days a week and bingo on the others. In 1972 the Cybi obtained a licence to operate as a Bingo and Social Club but by 1980 the licence was given up. For the next few years the hall was hardly used so it was boarded up. By today the Cybi has a new use as Unemployed Workers Centre.

The Cybi Hall, Holyhead as it is today

29. Holywell, Flintshire

Holywell is famous for its healing waters and its association with St Winifred.

First indication of film showing dates back to 1911/12 when the town was visited by the travelling showmen and their electric bioscope.

Empire Palace began showing films regularly in 1914; the 750 seat cinema operated by P N Whiteside. According to Kinematograph Year Book it was renamed to **Prince of Wales Theatre/Cinema** in early 1920s and run by J F Burns and M Clegg. There was one show per night with two changes per week. Fitted originally with the Cambriaphone sound system but was replaced by Western Electric in 1940 when the cinema was taken over by Paramount Pictures. A Mr H Watson took over the control of the cinema in 1950 and was renamed the **Rialto Cinema**. The cinema was fitted with a 20 foot screen in 1955 but due to poor attendance closed in early 1960s and became a supermarket in the mid-sixties.

The army camp at Kinmel Bay located near Bodelwyddan castle was opened in 1915 but the army had used the site prior to that. Most of the camp buildings were of timber construction while the corrugated building was added between the wars. The first cinema was located in the YMCA building but the actually **Globe** cinema was built in the thirties and eventually ran by the AKC (Army Kinema Corporation) in 1958. It was equipped with Kalee projectors and Western Electric sound system. The venue had a seating capacity for 200 plus seats. The cinema was run by civilians on behalf of the AKC. The cinema and camp closed in 1974 and by the end of the decade most of the camp buildings were demolished.

Army personnel about to enter the Globe Cinema, Kinmel Bay Camp

Army Kinema Corporation Globe Cinema on the camp

Interior of the Globe Cinema, Kinmel Bay (SKC)

31. Llanberis, Gwynedd

Today Llanberis is the terminus of the Snowdon Mountain Railway and the tourist attraction of Electric Mountain and Llyn Padarn, but the area grew to prominence with slate quarries. With a large number of workers the town soon grew and entertainment became important.

The **Empire** was the first of the purposely built cinemas in the town which opened in 1918 with seating of 250 and had a proscenium of 18 feet. It was registered as equipped with Electrochord sound system in 1928 the proprietor was Mr C S Wakeham. It showed one nightly performance at 7pm with two changes per week. By 1950 the cinema had closed.

Concert Hall began showing films with Uniquephone sound system in 1934 but closed 1956. It was re-opened again as a cinema by C S Wakeham in 1956. The hall had a 23 foot proscenium and a 19½foot screen, seating capacity was for 285, but due to poor attendance closed in 1961.

32. Llandudno, Conwy

Llandudno the famous Victorian seaside resort on the north Wales coast was once renowned for its entertainment venues and especially cinemas, but by today there is not one cinema in the town, the nearest is at Llandudno Junction some miles from the town.

Llandudno was the home of one of Wales' early cinema pioneers John Codman son of the Punch and Judy maestro who toured north Wales with his living picture show in 1905 from his base on Llandudno pier.

The **Grand Theatre** designed by Edwin O Sachs on Mostyn Broadway was built towards the end of the 19th century and opened on Bank Holiday Monday 5th August 1901. Built as theatre with a plain brick frontage but had a lavish interior seating 1,100 in three tiers. The first films shown at the theatre was around 1922 with the projection box situated in the dress circle. Three shows were shown daily with a change of programmes every Monday and Thursday when there was not a live show. With the introduction of the 'talkies' a British Acoustic sound system was installed. During the Second World War the theatre became under the control of the BBC which used the theatre as a radio studio for concerts. After the war the Grand was mostly used for live performances. The Grand Theatre closed when Venue Cymru opened in 1980. It was acquired in 1987 and reopened as the night club the Broadway Boulevard. The stall area was removed and a false roof installed. The night club closed in June 2013 but was acquired in 2015 and together with a Grand Theatre Trust are trying to preserve and restore the building to provide films and live shows.

A purpose built entertainment venue **St George's Hall** on Mostyn Street was built in 1864 to cater for the large influx of visitors coming to the resort. Initially built as a concert house and theatre on one level (a balcony was added later) it first hosted film shows in February 1911 with Mr W Watson as the operator. Short films were shown regularly together with the revues at the theatre until the 1920s. In August 1911 the venue changed its name to the **Princes Theatre**. In 1920 it was classed as a cinema with three shows daily changing twice a week. With the coming of the

1 The Grand Theatre on Mostyn Broadway also showed films; 2. The circle and boxes at the Grand Theatre; 3. St Georges Hall/Princes Theatre also was used for film showing (Silver Screen Archives); 4. Crowds outside the Princes Cinema/St Georges Hall

'talkies' a Western Electric Sound system was installed in 1930. By now it was known as the **New Princes Cinema** and after refurbishment it had seating capacity for 773 patrons. It continued to show films throughout the war years but in the fifties attendances declined and the cinema was losing money. As the result wide screen equipment was never fitted as in the other cinemas in the resort. The New Princes closed in 1957 and the building was sold to a supermarket group. Today the building is occupied by a HMV store.

In March 1914 the Llandudno Cinema Company was registered with the intention of building a cinema on land acquired a year earlier. The new cinema known as the **New Theatre** or the **Picturehouse** on Mostyn Street opened in August 1914. The Bioscope Magazine listed the venue as a 900 seat cinema, although some of which were just wooden benches. With the advent of 'talkies' the cinema was refurbished and fitted with RCA sound system. In 1931 Associated British Cinemas took over the lease of the cinema and a year later changed its name to the **Savoy Cinema**. After rebuilding the proscenium was increased to 27 feet and seating was reduced to 870. The Savoy continued to operate during the war but the cinema was seriously damaged in a fire in 1942. It remained derelict until 1954 when a new cinema was built capable of seating 600 patrons on a single floor which opened in August 1955. The proscenium was increased to 30 feet which gave the cinema a 24½ x 14 feet cinemascope screen. In 1960 the Savoy was sold to the Hutchinson Group and continued to run as a cinema until October 1986 but it remained empty until 1995 when it was converted into retail outlets.

The Riviere's Opera House/the Hippodrome/Arcadia were not regarded as a cinema. The long narrow 1,137 seat venue was built as a theatre. Although in its early years did show some films arranged by W H Taylor. By today the building has been demolished making way for the extension of the Venue Cymru.

The **Palladium Theatre** on Gloddaeth Street opened as a cinema in 1920. It was a three tier venue with a 30 foot proscenium and 30 foot deep stage with eight dressing rooms at the rear and side. The theatre could accommodate 1.440 people including four boxes on either side of the stage. The projector box was situated in the balcony and was equipped

1. *The Palladium Cinema on Gloddaeth Road (via Llandudno Archives); 2. Old print of the Palladium stage and auditorium; 3. Postcard showing the Palladium and the Odeon on Gloddaeth Road; 4. The Astra cinema was previously the Odeon and before that it was the Winter Gardens (via Llandudno Archives)*

1. The Savoy Cinema site today is retail outlets; 2. Today apartments stand on the site of the Winter gardens; 3. The Grand closed as a theatre when Venue Cymru opened and became a night Club; 4. Today the site of St Georges Hall is used by HMV

with Kalee projectors. A Western Electric sound system was installed with the introduction of the 'talkies'. The Palladium continued to show films throughout the war years. Throughout the 50s and 60s during the summer months, 'Summertime Revues' and plays were performed on the stage. Cinemascope equipment with a 26½ x 13 foot screen was installed in 1955 even some early 3 D pictures were also shown. Llandudno cinemas also suffered in audience down turn especially during the winter months therefore in 1960 the Palladium changed to bingo on certain nights and eventually in 1972 to a bingo/cinema entertainment centre with cinema in the balcony and the bingo hall in the stalls area. Like other venues in the area it was acquired by the Hutchinson Group. By 1995 it was run by the Apollo Leisure (UK) Ltd who had plans to refurbish the venue but never materialised. The Palladium closed on 8th September 1999 and remained empty until acquired by J W Weatherspoon who restored much of the theatre auditorium decorations to its original décor.

The **Winter Gardens** on Gloddaeth Street was built by Zack Brierley, a coach and holiday operator in the town and was opened 25th March 1935. The theatre had a 40 foot proscenium with a stage depth of 30 feet. There were 14 dressing rooms but lack showers. Initially seating capacity was 1,900 but after refurbishment was reduced to 1,079 in the stalls and 809 in the balcony. The art-deco building comprises of the theatre and café on the first floor with a dance ballroom on the ground floor. The theatre was used for both live shows and film shows. BTH projectors and sound system was installed from the beginning with cinemascope added in 1954. The theatre was also equipped with a Christie organ which was used during organ recitals until its closure. In 1936 the Winter Gardens was taken over by Oscar Deutsch's Theatres and was renamed the **Odeon** in 1943. Throughout the war it continued to show films and live shows. On 13th October 1969 the theatre was sold to the Hutchinson Group which renamed it the **Astra**. During the seventies it only showed films during the Summer Season. The Astra closed completely in October 1986 and was sold for development. It was demolished 1988 and by today the site is occupied by apartments.

Llandudno Junction, Conwy

Cineworld built a new multiplex cinema on the site of the railway carriage shed and sidings. The complex is equipped with 9 screens capable of showing both 2D and 3D films. It opened on 13th April 2001 and it's the only cinema serving Llandudno and the Conwy area.

The Cineworld multiplex at Llandudno Junction

33. Llanfairfechan, Conwy

There is evidence of an ancient settlement back some 7 thousand years ago in the Llanfaifechan area. It grew to prominence as a seaside resort with the coming of the railway.

The **Town Hall** was used as a cinema in 1920 equipped with Uniquephone sound system. The proscenium was 26 feet and a stage depth of 26 feet plus two dressing rooms at the rear. Seating capacity was 300. The hall was leased by Mr E H James of Llanrwst and became the **Town Hall Cinema** until 1936. There was one nightly show with two on a Wednesday and three on a Saturday during the summer. In the thirties Mr James company the Llanrwst Cinema Company renewed the lease on the building. In the forties BTH projectors and sound system was installed, replacing the Kalees.

The Town Hall and Community Centre today. Until the 1970s it was known as the Town Hall Cinema and the Luxor

According to Kinematograph Year Book the name was officially changed to the **Luxor Cinema** in 1945, although it was known as such for some years. There was a continuous performance each night Monday to Friday and three on a Saturday. The Luxor closed in 1956. Today the building is a community centre showing the occasional film.

34. Llangefni, Anglesey

A county town in the centre of Anglesey.

Town Hall was used as a cinema prior to 1920 by visiting film showmen.

Arcadia Hall a 400 seat venue showed films from 1920. The cinema had a 20 foot proscenium and a stage depth of 18 feet. The cinema was listed with T J James as proprietor and O E Hughes as manager, showing films three nights a week. British Acoustic system was installed in 1931. During the Second World War the cinema was taken over by Mr J Waterman's company, Royal Cinema (Amlwch). Cinemascope was introduced in 1956 with a new 22 feet wide screen was fitted in front of the proscenium. In the 1960s the Arcadia had been taken over by Messrs T J and D O Roberts who introduced bingo but closed in 1980 and the building demolished in the 1990s.

The Arcadia Cinema, Llangefni (via K Thomas)

35. Llangollen, Denbighshire

Today Llangollen is famous for its International Eisteddfod which attracts people from all over the world.

Pavilion was recorded as showing silent films in 1911 but by 1919 it had ceased.

Town Hall Cinema, 1928 was a multi-purpose building had a large stage of 20 feet deep and accompanied dressing rooms. Films were shown until 1931.

Dorothy Cinema, 17 Castle Street opened in 1933 had a small proscenium of only 16 feet, seating capacity 450. British Acoustic Sound system was installed. Cinemascope was fitted in 1957 with a 22 x 11 feet screen fitted in front of the small proscenium. The cinema showed films until early seventies when it continued to functioned as a multi- purpose hall.

Today a **New Dot Cinema** was established in Llangollen Town Hall, Castle Street with the help of BFI and was opened in July 2015. The cinema occupies the balcony and is equipped with a NEC digital projector. The cinema is run by a team of dedicated volunteers showing one film a month at the moment.

Entrance to the Dorothy Cinema Llangollen

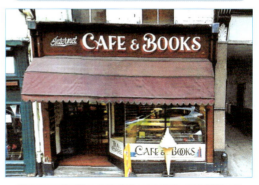

The entrance to the cinema today has been converted into a shop

36. Llanrwst, Conwy

Llanrwst is a market town on the river Conwy and some 15 miles from Llandudno. First recorded film shows exhibited in the town was early animated pictures by travelling showmen. In 1912 a certain Mr and Mrs Roberts applied for a Cinematograph Licence to show films in the **Concert Hall** above the old bank. Initially was refused as the venue it did not conform with the safety regulations, but after extensive alteration licence was given.

Years prior to the First World War the **Parry Picture Palace**, Reville Hall operated in the town. It was a small cinema, holding around 250 people and seemed remained open throughout the war mostly showing government released newsreel films.

The Llanrwst Cinemas Ltd was registered as a company in July 1927 and in 1930 bought a disused school on Watling Street converting it into a 200 seat cinema with Uniquaphone sound system. The **Electric Cinema** as it was called had a proscenium of about 20 feet in width. The cinema showed one performance nightly with two each Monday and three Saturday. It remained opened until the new Luxor was opened in 1938. The 1930 designed **Luxor super cinema** was designed by Sidney Colwyn Foulkes and opened on 6th May 1938. Film shown on the opening day was Deanna Durbin in '100 Men and a Girl'. This was the most modern cinema in the county with Holophone colour lighting system; it had a seating capacity of 503 seats with ample leg space. There was a 26 feet proscenium, a small stage area and two dressing rooms. When cinemascope was introduced in 1956 the screen occupied the whole proscenium. The Luxor showed the latest films of the time until it became uneconomical and closed in 1963. It was taken over by Kwik-Save and converted into a supermarket in 1966 and remained so until 1996. Kwik Save was taken over by another company who sold the property which was eventually demolished in 2004 and now the Glasdir rural hub has been built on the site.

1. The Luxor Cinema, Llanrwst was a very unusual design (Welsh Cinema History); 2. The Luxor Cinema closed in 1963 (via Gwynedd Archives); 3. Another photo of the Luxor prior to demolition; 4. Llanrwst other cinema was the Electric. The site became a bank but has now closed (Nerys Phillips)

37. Menai Bridge, Anglesey

Menai Bridge or Porthaethwy is the Anglesey side where the famous Telford suspension bridge connects the island and the main land.

The first entertainment hall was a galvanised iron building situated on the small pier. The **Pavilion** built in 1904 became the town's only entertainment venue. During the summer months several concerts were held but according to local adverts film shows were also shown during the winter months by travelling showmen like Arthur Cheetham and James Saronie.

A new venue was built in 1909 namely the Town Hall which became known as 'The Cinema'. The owner was Mr John Davis whom after the war offered the building as a War Memorial to the town. In 1920 it was leased to a Mr Lee who put on film shows on Mondays, Wednesdays and Saturdays. In 1920 Messrs T Clarke and Rigby of Beaumaris took over from Mr Lee and a year later was taken over once again by Mr Wilde who ran the cinema at a loss. The 262 seat cinema was equipped with Kalee projectors and sound system.

Mr G E H James of Llanrwst put in an offer to buy the hall and build a new cinema which was accepted by the council. The Town Hall cinema was renamed the **Luxor** in 1946. The revamped cinema had a seating capacity of 410 seats, the proscenium was 30 feet wide and the screen was 12 x 9 foot, but was increased to 18 feet 6ins wide with the introduction of Cinemascope in 1956. There were two shows nightly and a matinee on Saturday. In the fifties the early Kalees were replaced by British Thompson Hudson projectors. A Mr R Johnson took over the control of the cinema but due to decline in attendance the cinema was losing money and went into receivership in 1968. It kept showing films for another two years but closed in 1970. The council took over the hall as a War Memorial Institute. Since then the building has been used for a variety of purpose including storing lighting equipment for a nearby film studio.

The Luxor Cinema, Menai Bridge as it is today

38. Mold, Flintshire

The first cinema in Mold originated in 1920 but it seem that travelling film showmen visited the small town much earlier. The first Picture Palace was the **Assembly Hall** which had an 18 foot in depth stage that often held live variety shows. It continued to show films regularly until the Savoy cinema opened. The Assembly Hall claim to fame was the appearance of the Beetles on 24th January 1963. It continued as a Dance Hall and a special function hall until 1980 when it became a nightclub and eventually a bank.

Mold purposely built cinema was the **Savoy** which opened in August 1926. The 800 seat cinema had a proscenium of 30 feet and an 18 foot depth. There were four good size dressing rooms at the rear. The Savoy regularly put on live shows and an annual pantomime. Unusual for public theatres and cinemas the Savoy had its own generator as public supply was unreliable. The cinema was equipped with Kalee projectors and British Acoustic sound system fitted in 1930s. The cinema was ran by Mr Schofield's company the Mold Picture Palace Ltd. Cinemascope was fitted in 1955 which gave the cinema a 30 feet x 13 foot screen together with a more recent model of Kalee projectors. It closed in late 1960s and after some period the empty building was demolished and the new telephone exchange was built on the site. Most of the curtains and other equipment went to refurbish the Hippodrome in Wrexham.

In the 1970 a new Civic Centre (**Theatr Clwyd**) was built on the outskirts of Mold on Raikes Lane. As well as two theatres a 120 seat cinema was also included in the complex. The Cinema is equipped to show both 16 and 35mm films, but by today have been replaced with digital projectors.

1. *Assembly Hall/Picture Palace, Mold (courtesy of Mold Library); 2. Assembly Hall as it is today; 3. Savoy Cinema was opened August 1926 (via Mold Library); 4. Theatre Clwyd provides both films and live shows*

39. Nefyn, Gwynedd

Nefyn is small town on the north western coast of the Llyn Peninsula.

The **Madryn Hall** built in 1881 became the town's venue for film showing beginning in 1911. The cinema was run by a Mr Greenwood who did all the jobs himself from selling tickets to projectionist. It continued to show silent films throughout the First World War, including the war documentaries such as the Battle of the Somme and the Charlie Chaplin films were always popular. By the early twenties with the advent of sound, silent films became scarcer and in 1930 the cinema closed. For the next few years it reverted back to a community hall during which time the hall deteriorated. In 1963 after refurbishment the cinema was reopened by Mr David Sutcliffe showing 16mm films once nightly during the summer months until 1973 when the cinema closed. In 2006 the building was demolished and is now a car park.

Supreme cinema, Old Colwyn before conversion into a retail outlet

40. Old Colwyn, Conwy

Situated east of Colwyn Bay grew to prominence in the 19th century.

According to local history there was a cinema situated on Abergele Road called the Picture House around 1912/13 showing silent films accompanied by a pianist . There were continuous film shows most evenings of the week until 1914 when the building was destroyed by fire. Since then retail shops have been built on the site.

The **Picture House** was built in 1921 but was only registered as a cinema in December 1922. It opened to the public the following year with one show per night and two on a Saturday. The proscenium was 45 feet wide with an 18 foot wide screen, the seating capacity was 470.

It was the first cinema in the area to install sound on a Syntok sound system (sound on disc) in 1929 but was replaced by Western Electric system in 1931 especially after the company reduced their rental charges. With the introduction of the new sound system the Picture House

The cinema building today is used as a supermarket

was renamed in 1930, the **Supreme**. In the thirties the cinema was in control of a Mr Alan Milner but was leased to Advance Cinemas in April 1938. It was re-registered in April 1944 as the Old Colwyn Super Picture Theatres Ltd. Mr A T Arnott was registered as the last owner of the cinema before its closure in 1955. Cinemascope was never installed because the owner was not prepared to spend extra money for the installation. After closure the building was used for the manufacture of diamond styluses for record players but was eventually acquired by Kwik Save supermarkets. Today it is Coop supermarket.

41. Penmaenmawr, Conwy

Pemaenmawr overlooks the Conwy Bay with good views of Great Orme's Head. It grew to prominence with quarrying and tourism.

Oxford Cinema was established by Mr Harry Reynolds in 1918 was renamed the **Oxford Palace Cinema**. Two shows nightly were advertised in the local paper with four different programmes per week. The cinema was equipped with Kamm Sound System in 1929. The 326 seat cinema had a large stage of 21 feet deep and 2 dressing rooms but ceased to exist after 1939.

The **Crescent Cinema** opened October 1937 with Gyrotone system. The 600 seat venue had 30 foot proscenium and a 15 x 11 foot screen. In 1940 it was taken over by the Paramount Picture Theatres Group who installed a British Acoustics sound system. There was one show per night Monday to Friday with two on a Saturday. In 1954 Cinemascope was fitted but by 1970 attendances had declined and it ceased showing films. The building was used for various uses but remained empty for most of the time until 1990 was finally demolished.

The town's Crescent Cinema in a derelict state (Welsh Cinema History)

42. Penrhyndeudraeth, Gwynedd

A small village situated east of Porthmadog.

The **Memorial Hall** was built in 1926 to commemorate those who died in the First World War; soon afterwards travelling film showmen began using the hall on a regular basis. First used as a cinema was in 1930 when a Mr Griffiths of Harlech became a licensee and became known as the **Merion Cinema**. He installed British Talking Pictures (BTP) sound system. The cinema became part of Mr Guy Baker, Paramount Picture Theatres Ltd in 1945 and was licensed to accommodate 500. By 1954 the sound system had been replaced by British Acoustics system about the same time as Cinemascope was installed. In 1960 Paramount Theatres decided to withdraw their licence and lease and the cinema closed. The Memorial Hall was refurbished and reduced in size creating a multi-purpose building and the large projection room was converted into a meeting room.

Neuadd Coffa/Memorial Hall formally known as Merrion Cinema

A village is situated between the towns of Caernarfon and Pwllheli.

Memorial Hall (**Burrows Cinema**) the proprietor was Mr N Burrows showed films in 1920.

It was a 326 seat venue and had a stage depth of 21 feet. From 1937 it was listed as being equipped with Kamm sound system. As the newly built Plaza became prominent in the town the Memorial Hall stopped showing films and reverted back to a community hall, which it is today.

Plaza Cinema, Water Street built by Captain Pritchard was opened in 1935 showing one show nightly. It was fitted with Western Electric sound system. The Plaza continued to show films throughout the war years but was taken over by the Pen y Groes Cinema Limited in 1945. Cinemascope screen and lenses were fitted in December 1956. The 660 seat cinema closed 1962 and was seriously damaged by a fire a year later and had to be demolished.

1. Pen y Groes Memorial Hall. In the 1920s it was known as the Burrow's Cinema; 2. Plaza Cinema on Water Street, Pen y Groes (courtesy M Pritchard)

44. Pentre Broughton near Wrexham

The village is situated on the outskirts of Wrexham.

The first purposely built building as a cinema was the **Palace** opened in December 1936. Although built by Mr T Williams was later acquired by the Deeside Enterprise Company.

The cinema could hold 500 people and was equipped with BTH – A projectors and sound system. The proscenium was 22 feet wide with a small stage for live performances.

A separate company was formed to run the cinema called Broughton Palace Company. Later was integrated with the Deeside Enterprise which was based at the Plaza cinema, Queensferry. In the 1950s the Palace showed films twice nightly with a matinee each Saturday. Attendance declined even after changing the films three times during the week and by the sixties the cinema had closed. The building was converted into a small factory but it was demolished in the late seventies.

The Palace Cinema Broughton village

Porthmadog was an important harbour for shipping slate from north Wales to the rest of the world, today it has more or less adjusted for the benefit of tourist and yachting.

Pre- First World War several travelling showmen showed animated pictures and early short films in the town. The first cinema recorded in the town was in 1919 at the **Central Hall** (**Pen Swaig**) on Snowdon Street and ran by Messrs Hughes and Price. Regular film shows were given and the cinema remained opened well into the 1920s.

The first purposely built cinema was the **Coliseum** in Station Road/High Street in on 20th July 1931. The cinema was built and owned by Captain W Pritchard. The 630 seat cinema was equipped with **Kalee** 12s and Western Electric sound system. Just after the Coliseum was registered as Porthmadog Cinema Ltd, the Paramount Picture Theatres took over control. In 1956 Cinemascope screen was installed and the seating was reduced to 540. As it was the only cinema in the vicinity it did quite well throughout the 60s and 70s. To support

the cinema financially the management applied for a bingo licence for one night a week. This continued until late 1981, but cinema and bingo attendance declined and the cinema closed in 1983. A new company was formed, founded by the Porthmadog Chambers of Trade called Coliseum Porthmadog PLC. The cinema was completely refurbished and reopened on 6th July 1984. By now the cinema was ran by a dedicated squad of volunteers. Another series of refurbishment took place in the 1990s including extensive rewiring. New dual 35/70 mm Cinemeccanica Victoria 8 projectors were installed in January 1994. The cinema continued to operate but attendances declined and costs increased. In 2011 the cinema closed after 80 years of showing films. Reluctantly the cinema was put up for sale for £235,000 and was eventually bought by a property developer; however the demolition was put on hold because of bats in the lofts space. A save the Coliseum was put on Facebook. Unfortunately all the effort did not save the Coliseum and the building was demolished early 2016.

1. Porthmadog Coliseum Cinema in its heyday (Silver Screen Archives; 2. The Kalee projectors were replaced by 35/70mm Cinemaccanica Victoria 8s in January 1994 (via Dafydd Hardy); 3. The Coliseum was Porthmadog premier cinema; 4. No buyer was found and the cinema was demolished (via Daily Post)

46. Prestatyn, Denbighshire

Prestatyn is a seaside town grew popularity in the Victorian period and the coming of the railway. The town is also mentioned in the Doomsday Book.

James Saronie (Jim Roberts) was one of the earliest pioneers in film and cinema development had a close connection with the seaside town of Prestatyn. In 1898 he showed animated pictures accompanied by music and commentary on an Emile Berlina gramophone at Ty Caradoc School in Prestatyn.

The **Town Hall** was perhaps the first venue for any sort of film shows in the town being Magic Lantern shows and Dioramas as well as Cinematograph shows. As far back as 1909 such shows were recorded as taking place at the Town Hall. The magic lantern shows were included during the various piano concerts. In 1910 Saronie visited often showing sacred shows on Sundays. Within three years he had more or less taken over the hall and converted it to a permanent cinema. There was at least one performance nightly with a change of programme twice a week. During the First World War, Saronie showed a number of war films such as 'Battle of the Somme' and 'Machine Gun School at the Front' which was very popular and in great demand. In the late twenties the venue changed its name to **La Scala** and with the fitting of the RCA sound system on 8th March 1930 the audience was treated to their first talkie 'Broadway' starring Glen Tryon. As the result of the new wonder, prices were increased to the annoyance of the cinema goers. Also at this time the cinema was refurbished, the roof was raised, new seats were installed which increased seating capacity to 550. The stage was widened to 26 feet. A new frontage with the name in Neon Lights was installed which gave the theatre a new lease of life. The cinema remained opened throughout the Second Word War. Cinemascope was introduced to the cinema in 1955 which gave a 22 foot screen. With the retirement of Mr Saronie, the Scala was taken over by the Prestatyn Urban and District Council in 1963 and with a grant from the Arts Council the cinema was refurbished once again. In the seventies local governments were reorganised and the new owner became

1 The heydays of cinemas. Large que outside the Palladium; 2.People queuing outside the Scala Cinema in 1933; 3. Scala modern interior (Screen 1). The cinema was the first cinema in North Wales to install digital projectors (courtesy Scala Cinema); 4. The Scala today after an extensive refurbishment

Denbigh County Council. In 2000 the cinema was closed on safety issues as the council unwilling to rectify the problems. Friends of the Scala were formed who built up support from all walks of life throughout north Wales. However plans were drawn up in 2003 to convert the building to twin cinemas. After spending £3.4 million the cinema reopened on 13th February 2009 with modern interior and was the first in the area to install digital projectors. Sadly the cinema was still losing money and when the council refused to provide further financial support, the threat of closure rose again and in January 2015 the cinema and arts centre closed. Aurora Leisure who had a network of community cinemas throughout UK agreed to lease the premises and run it together with the local volunteers and was reopened later in the year. Today the cinema shows all recent releases as well as special theatrical productions direct from the West End in London.

Prestatyn's other cinema was the **Palladium** on the High Street which opened in May 1921. This was a multi-function building with a café, a dance hall and a 1,000 seat cinema. Although the proscenium was some 35 feet wide it only had a small stage. The cinema was equipped with BTH system which was installed the same time as the Scala. There was a one performance each night and a matinee usually on a Saturday, there was a programme change twice a week even after the introduction of the talkies. The cinema remained open throughout the war years. Cinemascope was installed in 1956 which gave a 26 foot screen although the seating capacity had been reduced to 622 mostly because of safety issues. By the late sixties attendances had declined and the cinema ceased showing any films but the owners Holyhead Hippodrome Ltd was granted a licence to convert to a bingo and social club. It remained a social club until 1977 when it closed and the site was sold. It was demolished in 1978 and a new Boots store was built in 1980 on the site.

47. Pwllheli, Gwynedd

Pwllheli is an important market town on the Llyn Penisula. The historical town dates back to the 14th century, but grew to prominence in the 19th century as a ship building centre and fishing port. Today it's a popular tourist destination.

The **Town Hall** in Penlan Street opened in 1900 with a live show- a pantomime 'Aladdin'. In the following year several magic lantern shows took place shown at the hall by travelling film showmen. By the outbreak of the First World War the venue had become the town only cinema. The premises was leased by C Lloyd Roberts for use as a cinema with one show per night but only when the venue was not required for live performances. 'Talkies' reached Pwllheli very late; an inferior sound system was installed in 1931 but was replaced by BTH system within four years. The cinema popularity grew with nightly performances increasing to two on Wednesday and Saturday. The Town Hall cinema continued to show films well after the town's other cinema the Palladium opened in 1935. The hall had a u-shaped balcony

1. Town Hall/Neuadd Dwyfor, Penlan Street, Pwllheli; 2. A view from the circle

1. *A travelling film show at Pwllheli early 1900s (Gwynedd Archive); 2. The Town Hall cinema continued to be the town main film venue for many years (Silver Screen Archives); 3. Aerial view of the Palladium which opened in 1935 (via RCHAMW); 4. The Palladium cinema, Pwllheli in its heyday (Eric Evans via Cinema Treasure); 5. Pwllheli Palladium Cinema was converted into a supermarket*

with good view of the stage and screen, the proscenium was 25 feet wide which was ample for a cinemascope screen of 24 x 11 foot when it was installed in 1955. In 1966 BTH projectors were installed in the cinema. The hall became the property of Dwyfor District Council in 1974 and was leased out to Mr Kenny, a former projectionist. In September 1993 the cinema closed for refurbishment which reduced the seating capacity to 354. In 1995 it was taken over by Gwynedd Council and renamed **Neuadd Dwyfor**. Today the venue shows up to date films on modern digital projectors.

The **Palladium Cinema** on Cardiff Road was opened on 15th April 1935 with the film 'The Camels are Coming' (1934). The 800 seat cinema was equipped with Kalee 20 projectors and British Acoustic Sound System but was replaced later to Western Electric sound system. There was a twice nightly film shows and a matinee every Saturday. Cinemascope was introduced in 1955 which gave the theatre a 35 foot screen but the seating was reduced to 700 seats and after refurbishment in 1975 was reduced further to 672 seats. By then bingo was also introduced on certain nights of the week. Cinema/bingo venue continued to trade until October 1977 with the last film shown 'When the North Winds Blow'. It was converted to a supermarket but in 1990 the supermarket moved to a new site and there were plans to restore the Palladium to an entertainment centre but was shelved. However the building was demolished in late 1990s and a jobcentre occupies the site.

Pwllheli other cinema was situated in the Butlin's Holiday Camp on the outskirts of the town. It was opened in September 1939 but during the war the camp became a Naval Training Establishment. It was continuously used during the war showing

both training films and feature films. After the war in civilian use the cinema was renamed the **Empire** and after the Rank Organisation took over all Butlin's Camps in 1980 the cinema was refurbished and upgraded which reopened in May 1980 as the **Odeon Cinema** and was equipped with two Cinemeccanica Victoria 8 with Dolby Surround sound system. The cinema remained opened for the holiday makers and the general public after the holiday camp was rebranded as the West-Coast World. The holiday complex was sold to Haven Holidays in 1997 and traded as Haven Holiday, Hafan y Mor holiday camp. The cinema closed in October 1998 and was soon demolished.

The Plaza Cinema Queensferry opened in 1936

48. Queensferry, Flintshire

Queensferry is situated in the middle of the Deeside industrial area. Its first cinema was a rented venue, the **Co-operative Hall** around 1910. Films were shown continually throughout the First World War. After the war the new lessors were Messrs Worrell and Price, but by 1923 the venture got into financial difficult and the cinema was taken over by G and A Davies and T Williams. Before its closure in 1934 the cinema was known as the **Gem**. It is believed that films were shown certain days in the week.

The first purposely built cinema was the **Plaza** on Station Road designed by the architect Sidney Colwyn Foulkes. The 600 seat cinema opened December 1936 with the film 'Rose Marie'. The brick façade with faience tiling below the canopy was built for the Deeside Enterprise Cinemas Ltd. There was a left and right staircase leading up to a small lounge. The auditorium was carpeted in red with matching plush red seats. There were two set of curtains a thick silver velvet with a gold fringe and the thin transparent curtains complemented by the auditorium's Holophane lightning system. The proscenium was 25 feet and the screen size was 18 feet x 14 feet, the projectors were Kalee 21's. Cinemascope was installed on 4th March 1965 with the first wide scope film being 'Lucky Me'. Performances were nightly with matinees on Monday, Thursdays and Saturdays most weeks. There were two separate shows on the Saturday evenings. In December 1967 Wedgewood Cinemas of Colwyn Bay took over the running of the venue but in 1974 sold the cinema to Mecca Ltd. It was closed for a year for conversion and reopened as a cinema/bingo venue with the cinema in the circle and bingo in the stalls. The cinema was opened Saturday evening, Sunday, Monday and Tuesday and bingo was on the other days including Saturday afternoons. The arrangement came to end and the Plaza was rebranded as a Cabaret Club, but closed again to become a snooker hall until 1990 when it closed and sold. It was demolished in the same year and is now a carpark.

This is a large village attributed to the rise of coal mining in the area.

Village Hall Cinema ran from 1913 to 1920.

Miners Institute also known as the **Palace Theatre** on Broad Street had a 750 seat auditorium and was built in 1924/6. The Palace showed its first talkie 'Golddiggers of Broadway' (1929) on 8th September 1930. The hall put on a number of live shows including the annual pantomime, film showing reduced to one day a week in the 1950s. In 1975 it ceased showing films altogether. It was refurbished in 1990 and is used today as theatre, arts and leisure centre known as the **Stiwt**.

Pavilion Cinema, also on Broad Street was a 900 seat cinema with a proscenium width of 23 feet. It was first listed as a cinema in the 1914 Kinematograph Year Book ran by the Rhos Pavilion Syndicate. Throughout the First World War it continued to show silent films accompanied by a pianist. Mr David Jones was registered as the proprietor but by 1939 the proprietor was the Pavilion (Rhos) Ltd. However it was taken over by NW & R Cinemas of Birkenhead. The initial sound system was BTP (British Talking Pictures) but by 1947 was replaced by RCA equipment. Throughout the war the cinema continued to operate with twice nightly shows and usually there were three changes per week. Over the years the Pavilion had several refurbishments especially the building façade, the final in 1930 when the front was completely rebuilt. The cinema remained opened throughout the fifties and sixties but due to poor attendances it eventually closed. Today the Hafod Colliery Club has been built on the site.

1. The Pavilion cinema Rhos near Wrexham in 1922 after some renovations; 2. By 1930 the Pavilion façade had been completely refurbished; 3. Today the site of the Pavilion on Broad Street is occupied by the Hafod Colliery Social Club; 4. The Miners Institute today is known as the Stiwt

50. Rhosneigr, Anglesey

The coastal village of Rhosneigr is located a short distance from the RAF airfield at Valley. Since Edwardian days it has been a favourite resort with holidaymakers.

Pavilion Cinema was a multi-purpose building which opened in 1920 showed films throughout the summer season with dances and variety during the winter months. The Pavilion had a small stage of 9 feet depth and a proscenium of 21 feet wide. In 1931 it was listed as having BTH projectors and sound system with Mr T R Evans as proprietor. However it ceased to show films in 1936. In 1945 the hall was acquired by a local business man Mr C W Beretta who refurbished and restored the building to its former glory. The 248 seat hall had a screen of 13 feet by 10 feet. Cinemascope lenses and a new screen were installed in 1956 giving a screen size of 20 feet wide. There was a one nightly show Monday to Friday with two on a Saturday. The cinema ceased to operate in 1960 and Mr Beretta sold the building to Rhosneigr Village Hall Committee for village use

The Playhouse Cinema, Rhos on Sea opened in April 1914 (Leonard UK)

51. Rhos-on-sea, Conwy

Rhos-on-sea situated between Colwyn Bay and Llandudno had one cinema the **Picture Playhouse** on Penrhyn Avenue which opened in April 1914. The purposely built building was capable of holding 450 people in a long narrow hall. It was designed by the well-known architect Sidney C Foulkes. The walls of the auditorium and the foyer were wooden panelled while the front of the cinema had a terracotta design with lavish ornaments. As the cinema did not have much height the projector box was only a few feet above the auditorium, but the floor slopped leading to a 27 foot proscenium and a small stage. In front of the box there was a musician's gallery. (Later was replaced with seating) In 1922 the owner of the cinema was Sidney Frere. There was a continuous film showing Monday to Saturday with matinees on Wednesday and Saturdays. With the advent of sound a British Talking Pictures system were installed in 1930 at the same time the Picture Playhouse was rebranded as **The Playhouse**. Messrs G H Lee and J F Buckingham took over the cinema in 1940 and installed BTH projectors and sound system which remained at the cinema until its closure. In the 1950s the Playhouse was refurbished and Cinemascope equipment was installed around 1956/7 with a 24½ foot screen which was quite impressive in a narrow hall. In 1960 Mr G H Lee became the sole owner of the cinema. Like most cinemas at the time attendances and revenue declined and the cinema closed in 1974. The building was taken over by the Co-op Society and converted into a supermarket. All the internal cinema features were removed and the floor was levelled, but the frontage has been retained.

The building is used today as a supermarket

52. Rhyl, Denbighshire

Rhyl was the leading tourist destination for families from Manchester and Liverpool.

In the years prior to 1910 there were numerous sites in Rhyl showing either slides or moving pictures such as the Bijou Theatre on the pier, the Queens Palace, Picture Theatre which was part of the skating rink, Grand Pavilion, the Gaiety Theatre and the Silvograph/Palladium. According to Kinematograph Year Book for 1914 there were six cinemas registered in the town the previous year.

By 1921 Rhyl had six cinemas showing continuous film shows throughout the week except on Sundays. The first ever moving pictures on a 12 foot screen appeared in Rhyl by Moore and Burgess whom introduced it into their stage show at the Winter Gardens in August 1896. Rhyl became the home for one of Wales's most famous early film pioneers, Arthur Cheetham. His first venue was the Town Hall in Wellington Street then at the Grand Pavilion by the pier entrance but was destroyed by fire in 1901. His next venue was the Lyric Hall in Market Street built in 1890 which had an upper hall of 60 feet x 20 feet and 20 feet high. The stage size was 26 x 15 feet and the auditorium could hold some 500 people. Also known as the Opera House as it continued to put on live performances. In May 1906 the venue was renamed **Silvograph** showing films only on Cheetham's silver painted screens. (Some screens today are painted silver) The Silvograph was taken over by Dick Shannon in May 1919 and renamed as the **Shannon Cinema**. In 1921 it was reverted to the name **Central**. In 1923 under Mr W J Churchill control the cinema was refurbished by rearranging the seating and decorating the auditorium and was renamed it yet again the **New Palladium**. It reverted back to Dick Shannon's control in 1925, but closed on 21st March 1931 when supply of silent films ceased.

The **Picturedrome** (also known as the **Kirk**) in High Street was renamed as the **New Picturedrome** in May 1911 with the silent film 'The Taming of the Shrew' (1911). The cinema was run by Mr Harry Kirk until 1917 when the building was leased to Saronie's Entertainment. In 1921 it was listed as The Super Picture House but closed within months to be reopened as the **City Cinema and City Super**

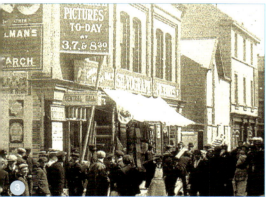

1. *The Palace Theatre/Cinema on Rhyl's Promenade was rebuilt in 1911; 2. Interior of the Queens Theatre Ballroom on the promenade; 3. Silvograph Cinema, Central Hall, Rhyl; 4. The Plaza Cinema on the High Street first opened as a cinema in 1931*

1. Central Hall cinema also known as the Silvograph in 1909 (Via Clwyd Archives); 2. The Odeon Cinema was also opened in 1937; 3. In 1968 the Odeon was taken over by the Hutchinson Group and renamed the Astra; 4. The Odeon Cinema taken in 1949 (via Rhyl history)

Cinema. Under the new owners Messrs Pontain and Barlow, it showed continuous performances with daily matinees throughout the summer season. In 1925 the cinema closed and was converted into a shopping arcade and was eventually demolished and replaced with shops and offices.

In 1911 the rebuilt **Queens Theatre** on the promenade was opened but it was later changed to the **Grand Theatre**. Initially the theatre concentrated on live shows but after the war was renamed the **Futurist** by its new owners. However, in 1921 its name changed back to Queen's Theatre and was the first cinema in the town to install sound system in 1929 with the showing of the film 'Showboat' (1929). Its owners Rhyl Entertainments Ltd commissioned S C Foulkes to redesign the theatre's interior and after extensive work the theatre was reopened in May 1933. The proscenium was increased from 18 feet to 26 feet giving a stage depth of 28 feet. There were also eight decent sized dressing rooms available. The theatre was equipped with British Talking Pictures projectors and sound system and had a seating capacity for 1,270 patrons in the stalls and balcony. Cinemascope equipment was installed in 1956. Revues and variety shows were performed during the summer months and films in the winter except during pantomime period. By late 1959 cinema attendances had fallen and the theatre was in need of extensive refurbishment so it closed on the 4th May 1960. Most of the building remains and has become a game arcade and retail shops.

Cinema Royal built on the corner of High Street and the Promenade was Rhyl's first purposely built cinema which was designed by Gilbert Smith for the Premier Cinema Company. The cinema opened on 20th May 1920 with the films 'Policy' and 'The Bat'. For the bigger films such as 'The Four Horsemen of the Apocalypse' (1921) in 1923 an orchestra was acquired to accompany the film. Western Electric sound system was installed in 1931. However on 4th February 1939 the cinema closed without prior notice. The site was sold and demolished and a Woolworth store soon opened. Today with the demise of Woolworth the store is owned by H&M. Sidney C Foulkes was once again commissioned to design a cinema on Rhyl's High Street for Rhyl Entertainments Ltd. Work on the **Plaza** began in 1930 and the cinema opened on 29th June 1931 with the film 'Mother's Millions' (1931) plus a full supporting programmes of films with local interest. The cinema was fitted with Western Electric Wide range sound system from the beginning. The Plaza had a seating capacity of 1,550 in comfortable surroundings, 900 seats in the stall and 600 in the circle and the auditorium was lit by Holophane lighting, Circle seats were padded and had arm rest which was a novelty in the thirties. The proscenium was 45 feet in width. When cinemascope was introduced in 1955 the seating was reduced to 1,505 to provide good line of sight for the patrons. There were continuous performances with a daily matinee. In late sixties the Plaza was taken over by the Hutchinson Leisure Group Ltd of Burnley who converted the circle to a cinema and the stalls as a bingo hall. By the 1980s even bingo had lost its popularity and the venue closed. It remained closed for some time eventually in 1990 it was converted into a shopping arcade, a snooker hall and a function suite.

In 1936 the Rhyl Entertainments Ltd decided to build a new cinema in the High Street. The **Regal** designed by Sidney C Foulkes opened 27th December 1937 with the film 'The Sheik Steps Out' (1937)

starring Ramon Navarro and Lola Lane. The Regal was equipped with Western Electric sound system. The 1,600 seat, 900 in the stalls and 700 in the circle had a proscenium of 40 feet wide enough for a substantial width cinemascope that was introduced in 1955. With the decline of cinema attendances and a sharp decline in holidaymakers the cinema closed in December 1962. The building was sold and eventually demolished to be replaced by retail units.

The **Odeon Cinema** on the corner of Brighton and High Street overlooking the railway station was built in 1936 and opened on 30th October the following year with the film 'Farwell Again' starring Flora Robson. The cinema was equipped with Odeon's standard equipment BTH projectors and sound system. The 1,408 seat cinema (862 in the stalls and 546 in the circle) showed continuous shows from 2.30 every day. In 1968 the cinema was sold to the Hutchinson Leisure Group and was reopened on the 13th September 1968 as the **Astra cinema**. It remained a one screen cinema until 1972 when the theatre was converted into a triple cinema and a bingo hall. Screen 1 with 750 seats, Screen 2 with 250 seats and Screen 3 with 225

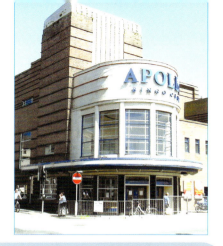

seats. The cinema reopened on 24th April 1972 with the films 'Under Milk Wood' (Screen 1) 'The French Connection' (Screen 2) and 'Nicholas and Alexandra' (Screen 3). In 1980 the Hutchinson Group was taken over by Apollo Leisure whom was at the time building a multiplex on the seafront. When the multiplex opened in November 1996 the Astra was de-tripled and was only used for bingo under the name Apollo Bingo.

The **Apollo multiplex** on the seafront opened in November 1996. It was built as a joint venture with the District Council who provided the building as it was part of the redevelopment of the seafront and Apollo Leisure ran the cinema. The 5 screen multiplex was equipped by Apollo. In 2009 Apollo was the first group to discontinue with 35 mm films and changed to digital system. Apollo Cinemas was acquired by Vue Group in 2012/13 and the Rhyl multiplex was renamed the Vue in 2013. Since then the cinema has been refurbished and is now capable of showing 3D films.

53. Ruabon, Denbighshire

Ruabon grew to prominence during the North Wales coalfield boom, but by today there is hardly any sign of the industry.

Parish Hall Cinema opened 1928 and was fitted for sound in 1932 initially by Excyclophone but replaced by Imperial sound system in the early sixties. The cinema had a seating capacity for 350 people. In the 1950s it was listed as having two performances Monday, Wednesday and Saturday with just one the rest of the week. In 1960 the cinema was run by GKH Cinemas of Ellesmere Port. As cinema goers were prepare to travel elsewhere to see up to date films attendance fell and the cinema closed in 1965.

54. Ruthin, Denbighshire

Ruthin is famous for its Medieval Castle and is steep in history.

Electric Theatre on Well Street a former boarding school and a factory opened in 1912 showing silent films.

Town Hall Cinema ran by Mr J H Brown opened 1924 closed 1929. The cinema showed three silent films per week until it closed.

The Cinema also known as Picture House Cinema on Wynnstay Road opened in 1929 ran by Mr G Davies had a 20 foot stage but a rather small proscenium of just 18 feet wide. There was one performance per night Monday to Friday with three on a Saturday. In 1940 the cinema was listed as having 375 seats with once nightly performance. This arrangement remained until 1946. The proscenium was widened to 21 feet in 1956. RCA equipment was fitted and cinemascope was installed in 1954 which gave a 21 foot wide screen. The cinema closed in 1964 but the venue was used for live performances and dances. Eventually the building was converted into a food store.

Site of the Picture House, Well Street, Ruthin

The Ruthin Cinema building has been converted into retail units

55. St Asaph, Denbighshire

St Asaph. Llanelwy in Welsh is the second cathedral town in North Wales.

Victory Cinema ran by the Walker Family opened in 1918 with two shows per night and a programme change twice weekly. The silent films were usually accompanied by a pianist, but it is believed to have closed within a few years.

The Alhambra Cinema, Shotton was built in 1921 and was opened a year later. The cinema closed in 1967

56. Shotton, Flintshire

Shotton not basic seaside resort nor a tourist destination but was more famous for its large steel works which by today has shut. During its heyday it employed thousands of workers whom lived in the vicinity and especially in the town.

The first cinema was films shown in the corrugated church hall. In 1922 a **Town Hall** cinema also known as the **Picture Palace** was listed and ran by Messrs Bullen and Broome Film Company and managed by Mr W H Cross. There were usually three different performances each week.

The Picture Palace prior to be converted to Vaughan Dance Hall and eventually Crystal bingo

This venue eventually became the Vaughan Dance Hall, Crystal Ballroom and Crystal Bingo.

The **Palais de Dance** on Plymouth Street opened late 1900s was used for dancing, roller skating and boxing tournaments but was converted into a cinema in the 1930s, initially known as the **Picture House** then changed it's to the **Ritz**. The cinema was equipped with BTH projectors and sound system showing mostly B films and older films. There was a continuous performance Monday to Friday with two shows on a Saturday. There was usually a matinee Monday, Thursday and Saturday. The Ritz had a seating capacity of 500 seats and a proscenium width of 20 feet. In 1934 the cinema was taken over by the Deeside Enterprise. In the early fifties attendances declined and in July 1957 the cinema closed. The building was sold to become a furniture store but when the store moved to other premises the building was demolished in 1997.

The other cinema in Shotton was the **Alhambra** built in 1919 and was opened in 1922 but started showing films a year later. Built as a theatre it had a 1,000 seat capacity with a balcony and two special boxes. The stage was 50 feet deep with enough height for flyers. At the side and rear there were six dressing rooms. The proscenium was 30 feet wide and had 21 feet by 18 feet screen. Latest BTH projectors and sound system was installed. Live performances also took place with the annual local pantomime.

Stanley Grimshaw Theatres took over the running of the cinema in November 1936 but was later leased to Byrom Picture Houses, then to a Mr Jacobs and eventually to Deeside Enterprises in 1945. There was a nightly performances Monday to Friday with two separate shows on Saturday. Cinemascope was installed in 1953 and admission prices were also increased. The cinema and theatre closed in 1967 and the building was sold to Tesco Stores who demolished it.

57. Valley, Anglesey (RAF camp)

RAF Valley built in 1941 is today the only military airfield in Wales.

Astra Cinema opened in late 1941 soon after the airfield was opened. Initially cinemas on military bases was only available to station personnel and their families, eventually it was available to local residents. In the mid- 1960s the cinema was reported as having a 25 foot proscenium and two dressing rooms, and was equipped with BTH Supa projectors. As other form of entertainment became available attendances declined and cinema closed in the early eighties, although it was used for other entertainment and renamed **Penrhyn Theatre**.

Penrhyn Theatre was formally RAF Valley Astra Cinema

BTH Supa projectors were fitted into most RAF Astra cinemas

58. Wrexham, Clwyd

As with most major towns in Wales, Wrexham benefited from regular visits by travelling film showmen who showed magic lantern and cinematograph films in various halls and fair grounds. Most were exhibit at the Public Halls and Corn Exchanges and the Empire Music Halls.

According to the Bioscope magazine Wrexham had three cinemas listed in 1911.

Wrexham Public Hall was destroyed by fire in 1906, however a new **Public Hall and Opera House** was built on Henblas Street. The new venue was opened on 1st July 1909 and was renamed the **Hippodrome** theatre in 1911. On 9th September it became known as the **Hippodrome Cinema** and reopened with the Gaumont British film 'The Donavan Affair'. In 1936 the cinema became part of the H D Moorhouse circuit but closed November 1959 with the films Jeff Chandler in 'Pay the Devil' and 'Star in the Dust' starring John Agar. On 13th June 1961 the Hippodrome was taken over by Barry Flanagan and reopened it with Pat Boone in 'All Hands on Deck'. By the seventies

The Glynn Cinema, Queen Square opened in 1910 (via Wrexham History)

The Glynn Cinema and the library in Queens Square Wrexham (via Wrexham History)

the stage area had been enlarged and several live performances were held at the theatre.

In 1988 the cinema was refurbished and twinned and became known as **Hippodrome Screens 1 and 2**. There was a great concern and objection at the time as the twinning spoilt the beautiful theatre's layout. Screen 1 was located in the stalls with a new projector box built and Screen 2 in the circle utilising the original box. By now cinema attendances had declined and the Hippodrome closed in March 1998. The building remained closed until 2004 when it was acquired by a property developer. On Monday 16th May 2008 a fire badly damaged the building and was demolished in April 2009.

The **Empire Theatre** on Lampit Lane was built as a Music Hall and Theatre in 1902. Films were first shown in around 1911. However it concentrated on variety shows rather than films. In 1914 it became known as the Empire Picture Palace. Mr Parkinson from Liverpool took over the cinema in 1930 but closed on 7th February 1932 with a variety show 'Rascal Magnets'. It reopened on 13th May 1932 with the 'talkie' film 'Let's Go Native' (1930) starring Jack Oakie. The venue could seat 582 patrons in reasonable comfort. The Empire continued to show films throughout the war years but closed on 26th August 1956. Several attempt were made to reopen the cinema but all in vain. Part of the theatre was incorporated into the adjacent pub, but the pub closed in 2011 and the time of writing still awaits a buyer.

The **Glynn Cinema** was located in Queens Square adjoining the library. Intending as a temporary building the Glynn opened on 23rd September 1910. Under the control of Mr J Langham Brown the interior was altered a little in 1919. A BTH projectors and sound system was introduced in 1930, although changed later to British Acoustic sound system. The first talkie film was 'Lucky in Love'. The fifty year lease on the building ran out in 1959 and rather than renew it on the temporary

1. The Majestic, Regent Street was originally known as Rink and Pavilion was often used for functions (via Wrexham History); 2. The Majestic building as it was in 2015; 3. The Empire in Lampit Lane originally was a Music Hall and Variety Theatre (entrance was next door to the pub) (via Wrexham History); 4. The Majestic Cinema, Regent Street (via Wrexham History

building the cinema closed 4th November 1960 with the film Steve Reeves in 'Hercules Unchained'. Soon afterwards the building was demolished and is now a car park.

The Majestic in Regent Street was initially built as a roller skating rink and a Pavilion which opened in 1910. Some films were shown together with skating and variety. The venue closed in April 1911 and reopened in May as the Rink Theatre. In 1920 the skating rink closed and a stage was installed and in 1922 it became known as the Majestic Theatre. Before talkies arrived films were accompanied by a live orchestra performing on the stage. The Majestic had 1800 seat capacity but this number was reduced later. The first talkie film shown at the cinema was on 15th December 1930, 'The Grand Parade' (1930) with Helen Twelvetrees. Later in the thirties the venue was refurbished giving the interior an art-deco decoration. The Majestic was also famous for their live show especially pantomimes. BTH projectors and sound system was fully installed and in February 1955s cinemascope was introduced with the film 'The Student Prince'. The Majestic closed on 22nd June 1960 with the film Robert Morley in 'Oscar Wilde'. The building was converted into a supermarket then a furniture store and finally into a J D Wetherspoon pub which opened on 21st December 1998.

The **Odeon Cinema** on Brook Street was opened on 13th March 1937 with the film 'Song of Freedom' starring Paul Robeson. As was common with the Odeon cinemas of the thirties it was built in the art-deco style. The cinema had a 1,346 seating capacity, 956 in the stalls and 288 in the balcony. The cinema was equipped with BTH projectors with cinemascope installed in February 1955 with the film 'Sign of the Pagan' with Jack Palance. A bingo licence was acquired in 1972 and alternated with the film showing. Eventually film showing ceased and the Odeon completely converted to bingo as the Top Rank Club from May 1976. The last film shown was Sean Connery in 'The Man Who would be King' on 15th May 1976. Today the building is a night club.

Odeon Plas Coch was a multiplex with seven screens which opened 4th December 1997. The cinema seating varied from 364 – 112 seats. Most of the

1. Simple entrance to the Hippodrome Cinema, Henblas Street; 2. The Hippodrome auditorium;
3. The Odeon Cinema on Brook Street opened in 1937; 4. Entrance to the Odeon just after its opening

equipment was 35 mm although a digital projector was installed in one cinema. The multiplex closed 12 March 2009 when the Odeon at Eagle Meadows was opened.

Odeon Eagle Meadows an eight screen multiplex was opened on 13th March 2009 equipped with digital and 3D digital projectors complete with Dolby sound system in all screens. Seating capacity varies from 225 – 115 seats.

The **Vogue Cinema** was situated above a public House, the Jolly Tavern on the High Street. It opened by Miss B Brookes, the district Euro MP in July 1981 with the film 'Tess' starring Nastassia Kinski. The cinema was run by Mr Barry Flanagan. The cinema was destroyed in a fire in September 1986 and has not re-opened. Today the building is a Chinese restraint.

1. *The Odeon Brook Street foyer (via RIRA); 2. The building today is used as a night club;*
3. *The Odeon multiplex Plas Coch had a short existence and now has been demolished;*
4. *Brightly lit entrance to Odeon Plas Coch; 5. It was replaced by Odeon multiplex at Eagle Meadow;*
6. *The lavish interior of the new Odeon*

COMPACT CYMRU
– MORE TITLES;

**FULL OF COLOUR IMAGES
AND CONCISE WRITING**

www.carreg-gwalch.cymru

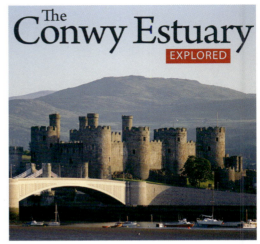

The
Conwy Estuary
EXPLORED

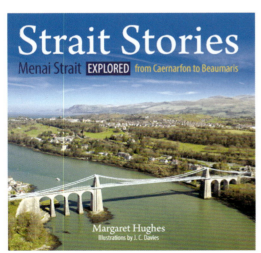

Strait Stories
Menai Strait **EXPLORED** from Caernarfon to Beaumaris

Margaret Hughes
Illustrations by J. C. Davies

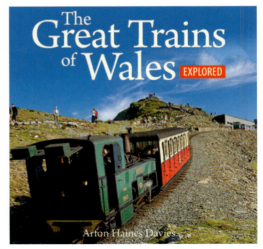

The
Great Trains
of Wales **EXPLORED**

Arfon Haines Davies